MW01640348

ALL BEING IS CONSCIOUSNESS

ALL BEING
IS
CONSCIOUSNESS

Selected Passages from
the Addresses of

WILLIAM D. KILPATRICK

The Bookmark
Santa Clarita, California

Kilpatrick, William D. (William Duncan)
All being is consciousness / by William D.
Kilpatrick.
p. cm.
LCCN 2005928147
ISBN-13: 978-0-930227-76-0
ISBN-10: 0-930227-76-X

1. Christian Science. 2. Consciousness—Religious
aspects—Christianity. 3. Spiritual healing.
I. Title.

BX6945.K38 2005 289.5
QBI05-600075

Published by
The Bookmark
Post Office Box 801143
Santa Clarita, California 91380

CONTENTS

vii
Foreword

1
All Being Is Consciousness
Association Address of 1932

38
Our Right to True Individualism
Association Address of 1934

86
Man — God Sustained
Association Address of 1944

100
Healing Is in Individual Consciousness
Association Address of 1941

122
The Practice of Christian Science
Association Address of 1928

147
The Infinity of God and Man
Association Address of 1937

FOREWORD

It is becoming well known that "all being is consciousness." Our thinking determines our experience. Mr. Kilpatrick goes deeply into this subject, showing how spiritual enlightenment can so transform consciousness that we can leave behind the cares and woes of mortal existence and emerge into a life of ever-increasing health and happiness.

Mr. Kilpatrick was a foremost teacher and lecturer in the Christian Science movement during the 1920's and 1930's, when the Church was at the height of its prosperity. He entered the healing work in 1912, and for over thirty years he was dedicated to serving the Cause. Each year he taught a class of thirty students, and held a one day meeting of his Association of Students, addressing them on the theme that salvation is in individual consciousness.

He brings out with "precept upon precept" the difference between the carnal mind, the human mind, and the divine Mind. He explains how we make our own world by the thoughts we let into consciousness. He emphasizes the fact that salvation is entirely an individual demonstration — one that can begin here and now to exchange carnal beliefs for spiritual ideas.

The Bookmark is fortunate to have obtained seven of Mr. Kilpatrick's association addresses, which are among the finest of any teacher's addresses to survive the ravages of time. The address of 1935, *Treatment*, has been published as a separate book because it is so outstanding. This book includes excerpts from the other six addresses. These have been edited, keeping only the metaphysical message of each address, because Mr. Kilpatrick was accustomed to sharing with his students his experiences as a lecturer traveling worldwide. His comments regarding conditions in other countries, in the government and the Church, and other remarks relevant to the time of the address have been omitted. The dark years of The Depression, and the threatening events in Europe in the 1930's have come and gone, but the metaphysics he gave for meeting such challenges are as suited to our own time as they were to those trying times of the past.

The metaphysics in this book are challenging, but as we come to understand the message that Mr. Kilpatrick is presenting, we realize how essential it is to carefully monitor the barrage of carnal and materialistic influences evident today. He explained so clearly the need to work even more diligently to close out the aggressive mental suggestions of animal magnetism by cultivating the divine ideas that spiritualize consciousness. Few early teachers have explained in such detail the influence our thoughts have over our entire experience. And, as Mr. Kilpatrick points out, only by replacing the material or carnal with the spiritual, will we find our salvation from all evil and learn of the kingdom of God within us.

ALL BEING IS CONSCIOUSNESS

Association Address of 1932

We must know God. That is our starting point, our guiding hand and our destination. We must learn to feel the nearness, the presence, the dynamic, vitalizing influence of the divine energy and being, and this can only be accomplished through the process of right thought. God is Love. Love is expressed in loving. God is with us when we love unselfishly, impersonally and purely. God is Mind. Mind is with us when we think Mind's thoughts. When we think Love, when we think purity, when we think kindness, when we think orderly, when we think unwaveringly, when we think truthfully, honestly, spiritually, hopefully, we are thinking with that Mind which is God. God is Truth, and we think Truth when we think honestly. God is Spirit, and Spirit is expressed in the spontaneous ever-presence of right ideas. God is Life, and Life is expressed in the activity of right ideas in our consciousness. God is Soul, and Soul is the divine consciousness of man. So when we are loving, fearless, pure, kind, selfless, spiritual in our thinking, we are thinking with that Mind which was in Christ Jesus. We are thinking with that Mind which is God. We are in reality thinking God. God is the only Love there is; He is the only Life there is; the only Principle, Soul, Spirit or Truth there is, and He is one. God is one.

All Life, Truth, Love are expressed how? In idea. Whence comes idea? From Mind. What is idea? Man. The idea of Life is man. The idea of Truth is man. The idea of Love is man. Truth is expressed in truthfulness. Truthfulness is idea. Life is expressed in activity. Activity is idea. Love is expressed in loving. Loving is idea. Soul is expressed in divine consciousness or thinking. Principle is expressed in law. Law is idea. Every time we express a right idea, we are expressing God. Idea is man. Therefore every right idea which you and I express in thought is man. It is a law of annihilation to everything unlike itself. Therefore every right idea which you and I express in thought is a treatment. Therefore every treatment is the expression of right ideas.

Divine Mind Source of All Ideas

Right ideas are man; therefore every Christian Science treatment is man. Man is inseparable from God. The only difference between God and man is one of quantity and not of quality. So do you not see how dynamic, how life-giving, how omnipotent your right thinking is? I am convinced that our failures or shortcomings in Christian Science are not due so much to lack of the letter or intent, but rather to the fact that we do not mentally endow our right thinking with the conviction of its omnipotence.

When we declare that twice two are four, it is an omnipotent statement with us as far as the science of numbers is concerned. We do not endow that statement with any sense of doubt or misgiving. We know it is omnipotent. This does not seem to be the case when we make a mental declaration of Truth. Our mental declarations of truth are clouded in doubt and speculation. There is so much of error in thought that the truth comes out grudgingly and reservedly. We must get to that point in our work where we can meet error with the sword of truth so convincingly that the question as to the result of our statements will not enter our thought.

God is Mind. Where is that Mind? How is it expressed? Mind is expressed in ideas, and ideas fill all space. Ideas are not the result of a thought process. In fact, ideas are not the result of thought. Ideas are expressed by man through the human function of thought; but this human function of thought does not exist in brain; it is a manifestation of consciousness.

Consciousness is the seat of all existence, good or bad, material or spiritual. The human consciousness may be either good or bad. When an idea comes to you or me, it comes because we have opened our consciousness to it. All right ideas are at this very moment ready to enter your consciousness. You do not have to think them into existence, to create them, to wait for them. They already exist, always have existed, and always will exist, and each and every idea stands at the door of your consciousness waiting admission. There is no process in the realm of ideas. Ideas exist as a spontaneous expression of Mind; and the very moment you allow a right idea to enter your consciousness, you are expressing the Mind of God.

An idea must come from some place. That is, it must have depended on something for existence. It was never created in reality. It always has existed full and complete as an expression of eternal intelligence, or Mind. Can you think of an idea not having its dependence on something? And could that something be anything less than God? And can you think of an idea which is dependent on a creative Principle as inseparable from that Principle? Therefore, could you imagine an idea as separate from God? It would be impossible to conceive of an idea as separate from its creative Principle. Therefore, when we express in consciousness a right idea, are we not as closely allied and united to God as the idea is? We must understand and appropriate this unity with God which right thinking brings, and through this we will be able to appropriate to ourselves the omnipotence which we give to God.

If man is God's expression, he must express Him in every particular; and if God is omnipotent, then our unity with God through expressing those ideas which originate in God, endows us with that same omnipotence. We fail in our demonstrations of Christian Science because we do not appropriate to ourselves that which our right thinking entitles us to. We are afraid we will claim too much for ourselves, and encroach upon God's prerogatives by assuming the God-power. We curtail and belittle our own endeavors by fearing to assume the position of God's sons which our right thinking places us in. The son of God, or Jesus, accomplished his wonderful works because he knew that he was God's witness; and as God's witness, he must of necessity express the omnipotence of God.

There is no separating an idea from God. An idea is omnipotent; there is nothing opposed to it. Therefore when you and I express a God-idea in consciousness, we are taking to ourselves the omnipotence of God. God is the parent Mind, the intelligence in which originates all things. In Science, all things are ideas. There is nothing to God's creation but ideas. Therefore an idea is a son of God. When we express in consciousness a right idea, we are sons of God. And every idea is endowed with the power and completeness of God. There is no difference between God and man except that God is the whole and man is a part. There is just as much omnipotence in one kind thought or one good deed as there is in a dozen kind thoughts or a dozen good deeds. Omnipotence is omnipotence whether it be in large or small quantities.

So you and I must learn to endow our right thinking with the omnipotence which belongs to it. We must appropriate to ourselves the grandeur, freedom and power which Jesus appropriated to himself. The same right ideas which enabled Jesus to accomplish what he did, are yours and mine here today. There is no more omnipotence in the thinking of Jesus, no more power to heal and to save, than in your and my right thinking. The omnipotence of a right idea which you or I or Jesus expressed comes from Omnipotence itself. The idea carries in itself and with itself all the power there is. It carries this power because it is the expression of the infinite Omnipotence. A right idea is God's power expressed.

Ideas Omnipresent and Omnipotent

Neither Jesus, nor you, nor I, could endow a right idea with any more power than it already has; neither can Jesus, you, nor I take away that power; but there must be some reason why a right idea in the consciousness of the Master could heal the sick instantaneously while the same idea present in your consciousness or mine seems to be less potent and less able to heal in many cases.

God is Mind. We know that, because He is expressed in

idea, and an idea has to have a Mind to originate it. Man, you or I, never created an idea. We express ideas in consciousness. Those ideas do not come from within us. They exist for our use, and we may appropriate them or reject them just as we please. We do not get them from anywhere, as a matter of fact. They are ever ready here and now, everywhere, filling all space, waiting to be expressed in our consciousness. You and I never created love, or kindness, or honesty, or constancy, or the like. These exist as one in the divine Consciousness and are expressed individually as we appropriate them to our own use. That is, Love exists as one Love. There are not many Loves; there is but one Love, and that one Love is expressed by you and me through an idea of Love. There can be a countless number of ideas of Love, but there is, nevertheless, the one infinite Love. The same may be said of honesty, justice, purity, etc. There is but one of every quality, synonym, or attribute of God.

Sight, for instance, is an expression of Life. Therefore sight is idea. There is but one sight, and that one sight is expressed in idea. When you are expressing in consciousness the idea of sight and endowing it with the omnipotence of God, you are overcoming the beliefs of the carnal mind which says that sight can be impaired. Hearing is a part of Life. Life is God. There is but one Life; therefore there is but one hearing. Man has no hearing of his own to be injured, impaired, or destroyed. Hearing is of God; therefore hearing is one. There is but one hearing, and it is perfect, indestructible and eternal, and is expressed as idea. Therefore, when you and I can clearly see that hearing is idea and not subject to any of the ills with which the mortal sense of hearing is harassed, we can begin to endow hearing with the omnipotence of God, and can meet the arguments which mortal mind attributes to hearing.

Hearing and seeing are ideas, and come from God or are a part of God, and therefore are not inherent in matter or physical form. Not being subject to matter or physical form, they cannot be affected by matter. An idea cannot be injured by matter. An idea is not subject to accident, disintegration, decay or old age. Idea is of

God, and is as omnipotent and eternal as God. Nothing of a material nature can interfere with the statement that twice two are four. That is true and changeless, beyond age, time, decay, or accident. And so with seeing and hearing. They exist as idea, and are as free from matter's whims as are twice two is four.

Individualizing Divine Ideas

Ideas existing outside of man, eternal in the divine Consciousness, standing ever ready at the door of our consciousness, knocking for admission, may be accepted or rejected by you and me at will. In the degree that we admit these ideas to consciousness and govern our activities by them, we are becoming children of God. As we become heirs of the promise, we inherit all the power belonging to God. Man must be as powerful as God if he is a reflection of God. We get the true sense of omnipotence when we eliminate in our thinking the possibility of any lesser power and conceive of God as the only power.

If there is a lesser power than God over which God has dominion, then God is not all-powerful. The sense of omnipotence in connection with God must be understood in the sense of "all" or "only" and not in the sense of "greater." If we can clearly perceive that God is the only power, we are free of the sense of struggle in our metaphysical work; and rest calmly in the assurance of our right thinking. Our expression in thought of right idea is not merely overcoming the sense of evil, but is eliminating the sense that there is evil to be overcome. The main object of all our work should be to rid ourselves of the thought that evil is real, for then we can rest, assured that there is nothing to overcome, and that the idea which we express in thought is the only power. But still there must be some reason why the right ideas which you and I express in our thinking are not accompanied with the instantaneous healing evidence which these same ideas accomplished when expressed by Jesus.

We have seen that God is Mind, that Mind includes all Life, Truth, Love, Principle, and that we in our present state of consciousness may accept or reject in our thinking these ideas which unite us with God and His omnipotence. We also know that this Mind is one, and that we reflect this one Mind by expressing that Mind's ideas. We may express many different ideas in our daily thinking, but nevertheless they all come from the one Mind. Mind originates all ideas, and these ideas exist in countless numbers, so that we can never exhaust the infinite supply of these ideas. Furthermore, it does not make any difference how many of these ideas we express, our identity remains because all the ideas which we reflect come from the same Mind.

Universal Carnal Mind and Universal Divine Mind

Love assumes individual identity as it is individualized. Just as God exists as one infinite Mind, outside you and me, so *the mortal mind claims existence as the mind outside you and me, and exists as one.* This one mortal mind becomes individual as we admit it to our consciousness. The admission of this mortal or carnal mind to individual consciousness constitutes our personality. Hate, anger, revenge, selfishness — all the claims of mortal mind — exist as one outside mortal man, but *these qualities of mortal thought become individualized or personalized by their admission to individual consciousness.* So just as you and I have the privilege of accepting or rejecting the divine Mind into consciousness, so we have the privilege of accepting or rejecting the carnal mind into consciousness. Thus we see that there is a state of mind which may contain some of the carnal and some of the divine. This state of consciousness — this mixture of both the mortal and immortal — may be called the *human consciousness*. Mrs. Eddy, in a few instances, has made the distinction between the human mind and the mortal mind; but in many instances she uses mortal and human interchangeably. In our present state of existence, there is the claim that consciousness may be a mixture of both good and bad, and this claim of existence may be called the human consciousness for the want of a better name.

Consciousness, we will say (and consciousness may be called mortal man), represents one hundred percent. You and I each represent one hundred percent, and that is made up of matter, sin, evil, goodness, and so on. All mixed together in mortal man are matter, sickness, health, harmony, inharmony, love, hate. It is perfectly obvious to a Christian Scientist that all of these qualities or conditions could not possibly exist together. Love could not exist where there is hate; health could not exist where there is sickness, and so on. But nevertheless mortal existence claims mortal man to be one hundred percent of all of these various things. It might claim that you and I individually represent fifty percent of evil, fifty percent of good, all of which make one hundred percent. Mortal man represents one hundred percent of all of the things which Christian Science proves cannot exist together with the divine. Human consciousness, then, may be termed the state of existence wherein good and evil seem to exist together in one human being.

As we shall see, all matter, evil and sickness is mortal mind, and all goodness or spirituality is divine Mind. These two minds seem to exist together in one individual, and this seemingly inconsistent existence is termed human consciousness. The human consciousness then is composed of both the mortal mind and the immortal Mind. Inasmuch as both the mortal mind and the immortal Mind exist apart and outside mortal man, we can see how optional it is as to what percentage of the mortal shall be included in our consciousness, and what percentage of the divine may be included. It is up to us to choose, to accept or reject that which comes to us of either mind. Divine Mind comes to our consciousness for acceptance in the form of ideas. Mortal mind comes to us for acceptance in the form of mortal or carnal thoughts. One is idea, one is thought, and you and I may accept or reject either at our own will. The percentage of mortal thought we accept represents the percentage of the carnal in our consciousness. The percentage of the divine which we accept into thought represents the percentage of the divine in our consciousness. So we ourselves regulate these percentages, and we determine the state of our own human consciousness.

Our Thinking Creates Our Experience

As we have learned in Christian Science, our consciousness constitutes our world. Our material world is made up of what we hold in consciousness. Our world is not made up of matter, sin, sickness, discord from without. Our material world is made up of our own thoughts. What you and I see, feel, taste, smell, hear and experience, are creations of our own thinking. You and I are conscious of a material world simply because we have thought that material world into existence. The material world does not exist because of any force or creation outside mortal man. The material world is a creation of mortal mind expressed through mortal man. What you and I experience is simply what exists in our thought. Mortal thought comes from the mortal mind which exists outside of human consciousness.

Mortal mind claims to exist as one mind outside human consciousness, just as divine Mind exists as one Mind outside of man. We may think just as we choose to think. We may accept or reject both the mortal and the immortal in our thinking. This thinking constitutes our consciousness, and our consciousness constitutes our world.

Our world includes unhappiness, sorrow, fear, accidents, calamities, sickness, want, woe, poverty, and the like, just to the extent that we admit the carnal into consciousness. Our world includes joy, happiness, assurance, freedom from fear or anxiety, abundance, health, harmony, etc., to the extent that we admit the divine into consciousness. If our consciousness is ninety percent carnal and ten percent divine, then our world is ninety percent unhappiness, sickness, sorrow, grief, want, woe, poverty, lack and the like, and then our world is ten percent harmony, peace, prosperity, happiness, and so on. We make our own world by our own thinking, and we ourselves regulate that world for good or bad, depending on our method of thinking.

Matter, Time and Space Conditions of Thought

There is but one real influence — that is the influence of good; but to the extent that you and I admit that there is any other influence by permitting the thoughts of the carnal mind to enter our consciousness, to that extent does our world take on the dual aspect of the mortal and the immortal. God and His creation of ideas are the only reality. There is nothing else in the realm of the real but God and His ideas; but you and I create our own pictures of misery by admitting that to be real which is not real. Matter is simply a condition of thought. Because of his understanding of this fact, Jesus was enabled to pass through closed doors, to emerge from the tomb sealed at its mouth with a stone, and to transport, instantaneously, the ship across the Sea of Galilee. Knowing that time and space and place are concepts of the carnal mind, Jesus could transport himself and the ship he was in to wherever he wished to be instantaneously.

Jesus did not move the ship in the wink of an eye across the Sea of Galilee. His demonstrations of the divine power were not ones of process. In fact, his demonstrations did not involve process. They were the spontaneous results of his knowledge that matter exists only as thought, and that, therefore, there were no material obstacles to be overcome. They did not involve process, or time, or space, or place. His demonstrations were the overcoming of time and place and space which did away with the thought or process.

Whatever mortal mind undertakes, or presents as a condition or a fact, involves *matter, time and place.* Time represents that which mortal mind calls duration; it represents mortal mind's process of construction. Everything that mortal mind knows as a person, place, or thing involves the process of time for construction. It involves formation, growth, periods of development, maturity, completion. Everything that is real and true, everything that originates and has existence in the divine Mind, is here and now created, always has existed and always will exist, involving neither time nor place nor space. We can prove, (as we have many times) that matter is simply a condition of thought, by silencing thought. The very moment a man ceases to think, he ceases to be conscious of matter. Change a man's thought, and his concept of matter changes. A man becomes unconscious, we will assume, for some reason or other; what becomes of his material world? It simply isn't. He hasn't any world. His material world exists only in his own thinking.

Change a man's thinking by the process of hypnotism, and what becomes of his world? It does not disappear. It changes. The hypnotist, through his belief in the power of mortal mind and his belief in minds many and wills many, and through the mental permission of his victim or subject, may enter the mentality or consciousness of another and replace his thinking with that of the hypnotist. He can, through his false beliefs and those of the subject, inject his thinking into the consciousness of his victim to the complete exclusion of any thought the victim may have. In fact, a hypnotist may think for another, showing conclusively that mind is not in the brain of an individual. Mrs. Eddy, in explaining the operations of mortal mind or animal magnetism, refers to this power of the hypnotist and shows how frail a thing mortal mind is. She writes in the Christian Science textbook, *Science and Health with Key to the Scriptures*, "The Christian Scientist demonstrates that divine Mind heals, while the hypnotist dispossesses the patient of his individuality in order to control him. No person is benefited by yielding his mentality to any mental despotism or malpractice."

The hypnotist, entering with his own thought the thought or mentality of another, and substituting his own thinking for that of another, may cause the victim to see an entirely different world from that which you and I might see under the same circumstances, or in the same place. The hypnotist may suggest anything to his victim with the result that the victim will believe it to be a part of his experience or world. The victim of a hypnotist may be made to think that he is existing in a frigid climate in mid-summer. He may be made to think he is suffering physical pain or enjoying physical pleasure when neither of those conditions exist. He may be made to believe that land is water and that water is land. And his conviction as to these conditions is just as real to him as your or my conviction that what we see is true.

There is no difference in reality between the convictions of the victim of the hypnotist, the convictions of the demented person, and our convictions right here and now. There is no difference in cause or effect between the hallucinations of the demented, the misconceptions of a hypnotized person, and our convictions, here and now. The world that we are conscious of as animate or inanimate matter is no more real than the belief of the demented person that he is a reincarnation of Napoleon Bonaparte, or the conviction of the hypnotized person that he is suffering bodily pain without a cause. The intense and agonizing pain which the hypnotized person may momentarily be conscious of, is no more real than any pain which we might experience in our sane moments. The pain which we might experience as a result of a cut, a bruise or a fracture, is no more in matter than the pain suffered by the victim of the hypnotist. There is no pain in either case. The thought is the cause in both instances. And where does that thought come from? Not from within us because, as we know, mortal mind does not exist within mortal man. Mortal thought comes from without. It comes from what we call the one carnal mind which exists outside mortal man.

Animal Magnetism Defined

In the case of the hypnotized man, if the victim had a knowledge of Christian Science, if he knew, in fact, that there is but one Mind and that that Mind is God, outside man, never subject to any change or the claims of mortality, he could prevent the operations of the hypnotizer from having any control over him. By refusing to admit the thought of the hypnotist into his own consciousness, on the ground that there is but one Mind and that Mind is God, good, he could protect himself from the belief that he could be controlled by anything but his own thinking.

It is safe to say that, generally speaking, no one who is spiritually enlightened could be made the victim of a willful or professional hypnotist because he would refuse to recognize any power apart from God. Yet I think it would be safe to say that a large percentage of what we do daily and certainly everything that we see, feel, taste, smell and hear, are manifestations of hypnotism or animal magnetism in one form or another. In all her writings, Mrs. Eddy uses hypnotism or animal magnetism interchangeably in many instances. One is the same as the other. She points out to us that all material existence is animal magnetism or hypnotism.

In *Science and Health* Mrs. Eddy says, "As named in Christian Science, animal magnetism or hypnotism is the specific term for error, or mortal mind." So you see that animal magnetism, as used by Mrs. Eddy, is the same as hypnotism, and this term animal magnetism is not simply a usage of words. The term animal magnetism is used because it more properly and clearly expresses material existence than anything else. It rightly reveals the nature of the material universe. It signifies the nature of the material, its substanceless existence, the elusiveness of matter.

One definition of animal in the dictionaries is, "Pertaining to the soul or will." Animal is in reality derived from the Latin word *animus*, meaning mind. So while the word animal in one sense refers to animate matter or animal creatures, the basic meaning of the word animal, that from which it is derived, and whereby it receives the definition of mind or will as above given, is mind. So the word animal in its last analysis refers and pertains to the mental rather than to the physical. The dictionaries use very freely the term animal magnetism. It is not a word coined by Mrs. Eddy. It is her adaptation of the phrase that makes it unique and useful in outlining the mental nature of the material.

Magnetism in the dictionaries is described as "the power to attract; power to excite the feelings of and to gain the affections." So the term animal magnetism has nothing to do with matter. In fact, it leads away from matter into the mental, and gives us a clear and concise statement that matter is not material, but is mental or the outcome of mortal mind's power to attract. In the dictionaries, animal magnetism is used interchangeably with mesmerism, just as Mrs. Eddy has used these two terms. So with the understanding that the term animal magnetism means the power of the mortal mind or will to attract or to deceive, we can begin to see why Mrs. Eddy used this term to define all evil. Mesmerism or animal magnetism as the terms are used together in the dictionaries and by Mrs. Eddy, means the hypnotic state of the human mind which conceives matter, sin and evil as real. Animal magnetism, hypnotism, and mesmerism all signify the same thing. Animal magnetism, Mrs. Eddy has designated as all matter, evil, and error of every name or nature. She has done this because it defines the mental nature of all of these conditions. It brings out clearly, in two brief words, the fact that all matter and material existence, are a state of hypnotism or mesmerism; and that when the hypnotic state is broken, men will awaken to their true state of being, unfettered by matter or the claims of mortal mind.

Origin of the Carnal Mind

Where does this mesmeric or hypnotic state originate? Not from divine Mind, certainly. It must come from what we call the mortal or carnal mind, which mind exists outside of mortal man. When mortal mind is accepted in and dwells in human consciousness, that results in a state of hypnotism, and through this state of hypnotism or mesmerism comes the belief of intelligent matter. Matter existence then, is a state of hypnotism, and when the hypnotic state is broken, matter disappears. Therefore, our material existence is a state of hypnotism. That hypnotic state exists because we admit into our consciousness thoughts of the carnal mind which come to us from without and which do not originate within us at all. And because these thoughts do not originate in us, but come to us from outside ourselves, we see how material existence becomes a state of self-hypnotism.

We have the power within ourselves to accept or reject these hypnotic thoughts if we wish to, just as certainly as we have the power to accept or resist the suggestions of the professional hypnotist. The professional hypnotist operates with the carnal mind alone. He operates with that mind which claims to exist outside himself as one mind — the one which argues to you and me that there is matter, sin, sickness, poverty, and the like. Therefore, the mind which puts one person under a hypnotic spell and makes him believe that he is suffering physical pain without a cause, is the same mind that tells you and me that there is a material body which can sin, suffer and enjoy. As the mind which is used by the hypnotist is the same mind that makes you and me believe we live in matter, the effect in both instances must be the same. The cause being the same, the effect must be the same. Therefore, that consciousness which argues to you and me that there is matter, sin, sickness and death, is just as much a state of hypnotism as the consciousness which is manipulated by the professional hypnotist.

The hallucinations of a demented person are no more real, and are just as real, as the hallucination in which you and I think, when our physical senses tell us that we see, feel, taste, smell and hear matter. There is no more reality in this dream of matter in which you and I are now struggling than there is in the hallucination of the demented person. Both come from the same mind, and the effect in one case is no more real than the effect in the other case. So let none of us fool ourselves that we have an advantage over the poor fellow who is incarcerated behind the bars of an insane asylum. Our condition is the hallucination of what mortal mind would call a normal mind. The insane person's condition is the hallucination of what mortal mind would call an abnormal mind. They are both hallucinations. The hallucinations of the sane person are what might be called primary beliefs. The hallucinations of the demented might be called secondary beliefs. One is no more real than the other. The universe of a sane person is the effect of hypnotism in the first degree. The universe of the insane person is the effect of hypnotism in the second degree. The universe of the sane person represents the hypnotic state of the normal mind. The universe of the insane person represents the hypnotic state of a sick mind. The only difference between the two is one of degree. The only difference is that in the one case there is a sick mind, and in the other case there is no sickness. Both are examples or expressions of animal magnetism, hypnotism or mesmerism, as you wish, and one represents no more of God than the other. One represents a little more of error, and that is all.

Material Existence an Illusion

All material existence, then, is a state of mental illusion which Mrs. Eddy has called animal magnetism. Matter, everything that you and I see, feel, taste, smell and hear exists only as illusion, a dream. The experiences which you and I have in a sleeping dream are no more real than the experiences you and I have when awake. Material existence is a dream just as certainly as the experiences you and I have in sleep. They are both states of mesmerism, hypnotism or animal magnetism. One's body can suffer or enjoy in a dream just as definitely as it can when one is awake. There is no more reality in pain in the one instance than there is in the other. Both are manifestations of the one carnal mind claiming to exist as one mind, outside of man, belonging to no man, but common to all men. The very fact that this mind is subject to change or unconsciousness is complete evidence of its non-existence.

God never created anything outside of Himself. God never created what you and I have termed the carnal mind. Divine Mind could not create anything unlike itself, anything it did not know or contain. The science of mathematics could not include a knowledge of twice two equals five, and not including a knowledge of it, it could not create it or recognize it. Therefore anything that God did not create, or does not recognize, does not exist. If the carnal mind does not exist, then that which seems to result from this mind does not exist.

If matter and the material universe are the products of something that does not exist, then whence comes matter and the material universe? They do not come, is the inevitable answer. And if they never came where are they? No where. What, then, is material existence with all its sin, sickness, poverty, and woe? It is just an expression of that which you and I experience in a dream. It is unconsciousness or not knowing — *the absence of Mind.* You and I dream only when we are in a state of sleep. The dream we have in sleep is the same existence we experience when mortal mind says we are unconscious, and the dream of material existence is no different from the sleeping dream or the experience of unconsciousness. We speak of the experience of unconsciousness as a condition resulting when the mortal mind is completely silenced. They are all the same. They are all manifestations of unconsciousness. The sleeping dream, the waking dream and the belief in unconsciousness are all the same. One is just as real as the other, and one is just as unreal as the other. There is no difference. They all come under the one heading of animal magnetism, and all are conditions of unconsciousness because they do not involve the operation of Mind.

There is but one Mind. There is no mortal mind. Therefore anything that claims to result from mortal mind, which does not exist, is not; and it is therefore a state of unconsciousness, of not knowing. So our problem is not to deal with matter or mortal mind, but to become conscious of the facts of existence; to come out from our state of unconsciousness into the consciousness of Truth. We are concerned then only with the Truth and not with error. And when we can begin to see that matter with all of its arguments of sin, poverty, sickness, and discord, exists only as a state of unconsciousness, of not knowing, we can begin to cease to struggle in our mental work with a sense of opposition of mortal mind or material conditions. If error of every name or nature is simply a statement of nothing, then we cease to feel that we have to struggle with nothing, and begin to put in place of that which may be called nothing, the realities of the divine.

Awakening from the Mortal Dream

While, as commonly affirmed, our work in Christian Science is one of substitution, in its last analysis, there is nothing for which to substitute the truth. When we begin to accept into and entertain in consciousness Truth, or God, are we not then doing all that is necessary to accomplish what might be called a healing? When we begin to admit Truth into consciousness and express Truth in our daily thinking and living, are we not then awakening from what we have called our state of unconsciousness? Is there any other process of awakening? Could there be any other process? If God is the only Mind, is there anything else for us to do to become conscious of the facts of Mind than to think God ideas? We have nothing to replace. We have no mortal mind to get rid of. We have no material conditions to overcome.

Much of the labor and delay in our metaphysical work, I am sure, comes from this sense of process in our work. We feel that there is much of mortal mind to get out of consciousness before we can begin the demonstration of the divine. We are inclined to feel that there is much of mortality to unlearn, much purifying to undergo before we can demonstrate Truth. Not so. We should not be so concerned with the matter of the carnal mind, sin, sickness, lack and the like. We do not have to overcome them, for they do not exist. It is our state of unconsciousness that argues for the existence of these conditions. Therefore a condition of sickness, poverty, lack, limitation, or inharmony does not exist in reality. These conditions express a state of unconsciousness or the absence of

Mind. When we begin to admit into conscious thought divine ideas, we are, consequently, awakening from our state of unconsciousness, or, rather, we are becoming truly conscious; and as there is but one Mind and that Mind is God, we are beginning to be consciously aware of our own true existence — that existence we have always had and which we still have, and always will have.

So birth, growth, maturity, death, are not real conditions, but no conditions at all. Harmony is our normal state of existence. Health might be said to be included in harmony. Happiness and abundance are normal and eternal states of existence at which we arrive in the proportion that we become consciously allied to God in thought. So we must learn to work, not from the standpoint of combat, but from the standpoint of perfection — man's eternal and ever-present perfection. Our constant expression of right ideas in consciousness is our conscious existence, and our only existence; and it must be clear to us that in the proportion that we are consciously expressing God in thought, we are not overcoming sin; we are coming into the consciousness of the omnipotence of God and the nothingness of sin. And if God is omnipotent, there is no opposite. Our constant declarations of truth, our constant affirmation of our sonship with God, our constant consciousness of good only, is our existence, and it is the only existence there is, and this existence does not include sin, or sickness, or poverty, or discord. And this conscious sense of existence does not include the necessity of combating and working against that which does not exist.

Our Daily Prayerful Work

I am afraid that our work becomes complicated and devoid of fruitage because we become so involved with error in our thinking. We are wondering how we can handle this error and that error. Our consciousness of good handles error. We do not have to handle error. If you and I had to handle error, it would be too bad for all of us. Our work is to know God, to think God, to live God, and that is true consciousness. True consciousness is the only consciousness there is, and there being but one Mind and one consciousness as a result of that Mind, we do not have to struggle to overcome that which has no mind to originate it.

Let us get this understanding of true consciousness. Let us get the calm, unlabored, assured, peaceful sense of our work in Christian Science. Do not sit down to your daily lesson and your prayerful work in Science with a sense of burden, a sense of duty, or a sense of struggle or combativeness. Be calm, collected, secure, buoyant and confident. There is nothing to do but to know God. There is no enemy, there is no mortal mind, there is nothing to struggle or work against. There is no opposition to our work. We have not to struggle. The consciousness of Truth is our work. Our daily work should be to so come into the understanding of the ever-presence of the true consciousness that any opposite sense does not suggest itself as a possibility.

Our periods of work in Christian Science, our periods of prayer, should be welcome periods, not periods of duty or strife. They should be periods of rest — calm, exalted rest. Communion with God cannot be deprived of its fruitage. But the fruitage should not be our goal. God brings the fruitage, and our duty is simply to get God into consciousness. Our periods of prayer and thoughtful consecration should not be hurried or crowded by the duties and affairs of the world. Our periods of prayer and consecration should be occasions to look forward to with anticipation and joy. Nothing should be so dear to us as the time spent in thoughtful contemplation of God, and surely nothing will bring as much joy and peace and comfort.

Affirming the Truth the Key to Harmony

We do not, and should not, work to a particular end in Christian Science. Let us learn to let God have His way. Let us learn that all of this world, all of the struggles, strife, failures, sorrows, disappointments, thwarted ambitions, blasted hopes, and the like, even in Christian Science, is because we work to definite material ends. We outline. What do we outline with? Mortal mind. We could not outline with anything else, could we? God's work is finished, complete and perfect. Nothing can be new or novel to divine Mind. Nothing needs to be done to complete His work; nothing can be added to it or taken from it; nothing can be changed. Mind's ideas are complete. Mind is satisfied.

Then what is it that needs the process of change? What is it that requires something different? What is it that, in reality, requires demonstration? Why, nothing but the human mind. When we sit down to work for things, for a change of conditions, for money, for supply, for this or for that, what is it that is telling us what we should work for? It is mortal mind. It is the human mind that says we are sick, out of our right place or position, unhappy, poverty-stricken, and the like. Then is it not mortal mind that would outline for us what we should work for? that we should work for money? that we should work for health?

God, or good, knows nothing about these things. God, who is substance or supply, could know nothing about lack. God, or good, who is harmony or perfection, could know nothing of inharmony or sickness. God who directs, guides and cares for all His vast army of ideas, could know nothing about misplacement or displacement. So any attempt or effort on our part to work for money or place or position or health, is simply an effort directed by the carnal mind, and could not possibly accomplish anything. We do not have to work to demonstrate over twice two is five if we know that twice two is four, do we? We do not have to work to demonstrate over sickness if we are conscious only of God in thought. We do not have to work to demonstrate a position when we are so consciously allied with God in thought that we cannot conceive man as out of place or position. We do not have to demonstrate over lack or limitation when we are expressing Love's abundance in thought.

Constantly declare the truth about yourself. This constant declaration is instilling the God-consciousness to the extent that this

God-consciousness becomes your existence; and to the extent that this God-consciousness becomes your existence, to that extent are the claims of matter done away with. Know that you are *now* the son of God, dwelling in your perfect state of existence, in your right place, the full expression of the one and only intelligence, the expression of all substance, life, activity, true existence. God is Life; therefore God is Mind; and therefore, to the extent that you express that Mind in conscious thought, to that extent are you expressing and realizing Life. A loving thought is Life. Love is Life because Love is God. Therefore, as often as you hold love in thought to the exclusion of all else are you expressing and experiencing life eternal. "To know me is life eternal," says the Bible, and to know God is to think God. Therefore you do not have to overcome sickness and death to demonstrate eternal life. You have to demonstrate God in consciousness to demonstrate life. Purity, kindness, love, honesty, spirituality in thought constitute life.

Our Individual World Illustrated

Now, our world, our surroundings, our environment, everything we see, feel, taste, smell or hear, as we have seen, are material because of our acceptance into consciousness of the carnal mind. Matter is carnal thought, and our material world is our individual expression of the carnal mind. If we refused this very instant to admit any carnal thought into consciousness, just at that instant would we cease to be conscious of a material body or a material world. But the human consciousness must be conscious of something — it must have an object or an objective; and therefore it could not cease its process of accepting the carnal mind without something to take its place; and that is where the divine Mind comes in as the Saviour, or Christ. When the human consciousness begins to replace its mortal thoughts with divine ideas, then it is that the Christ is coming to human consciousness, or to "the flesh to destroy incarnate error." The mortal mind in our consciousness constitutes the flesh and all matter, and when the divine replaces or displaces the mortal, then flesh and matter are being overcome.

There is but one carnal mind, and that mind, as we know, exists outside human consciousness, and is accepted into consciousness at will. Because there is but one mortal mind, and because the material universe is simply the expression of that one carnal mind, and because you and I accept into consciousness that one mind, you and I see the same material world. Your world is your world because it is an individual expression of your own thinking. My world is my world because it is an individual expression of my own thinking. But inasmuch as we both use the same carnal mind to create our material universe, we are conscious of the same material world; that is, while our worlds are each separate, and individual, yet they are the same because they were created by the same mortal mind admitted to individual consciousness.

Take for example this table before me. There are as many tables here as there are people here today — to illustrate the statement that each one of us creates his own material world. Matter is simply a state of mind. It is a state of the carnal mind, and to the extent that you and I admit the carnal mind into consciousness, are we conscious of matter. Now, I admit into my consciousness the carnal mind, and I become conscious of this table. This table would not be here as far as I am concerned unless I admitted to consciousness the one carnal mind. You admit into your consciousness the carnal mind, and you are conscious of this table. Now the carnal mind which you admit into consciousness is the same carnal mind that I admit into consciousness, and for that reason our concepts of this table are the same. If neither of us admitted to consciousness anything of the carnal mind, neither of us would be conscious of this table, and for that reason each of us sees his own individual concept of table. Each of us creates his own individual concept of table with his own thinking, and therefore there are as many tables here as there are mentalities to create them.

Each of us creates his own universe of matter by his own thinking, and there are as many worlds as there are people. I hope

I have made myself clear on this. It is important to be clear because it is a vital point in metaphysics. Only by understanding this, are we able to see how completely individual is salvation, how to rule out of our lives the inharmony and misery of the carnal, and replace the carnal with the divine.

If our material world is simply the expression of the carnal mind in our individual thinking, then the only way we are ever going to change that world from the carnal to the spiritual is to change our thinking. We create our own worlds by our own thinking; and that world is wholly material if we hold only the carnal in consciousness; and it is partly material and partly spiritual in the degree that we allow the spiritual to replace the carnal. So do you not see that no one else on the face of this earth can ever usher us into the kingdom of heaven, or ever help us to bring out a harmonious state of existence here and now? The carnal mind which you and I hold or admit into consciousness, not only enables you and me to see, feel, taste, smell and hear matter; but it enables you and me to see man as sinful, sick, poverty-stricken, and unhappy.

The carnal mind which you and I admit into consciousness enables you and me to see an accident, a disaster, a panic. It enables you and me to be conscious of unemployment, unhappiness, and the like. And to the extent that you and I are able to be conscious of an accident to others, or unemployment, to that extent are we ourselves subject to sickness, accidents, hard times, unemployment. We not only create matter with our own thinking, but with that same thinking, we endow that matter with the ability to be sick, to be injured, to lack, to be poverty-stricken. So do you not begin to see that enormous responsibility which rests on each one of us in the great scheme of salvation?

We could not be conscious of sickness either in ourselves or in others if it were not for the carnal mind entertained by us in individual consciousness. We could not be conscious of poverty, accidents, calamities, unemployment, in ourselves or in others if it were not for the carnal mind entertained by us in individual consciousness. Our individual bodies are our individual consciousness. Body is consciousness (material body). Our body is material because of our consciousness. Our body is sick because of our consciousness. Just as the man of God's creating is a compound idea of all right ideas, so mortal man may be said to be a compound expression of all carnal thoughts. Therefore every erroneous thought, every bit of the carnal mind which we hold in consciousness, is a part of our body. So we cannot hold sick or sinful thoughts in consciousness without making them a part of our body or our world.

Home is simply the compound expression of our own thinking. It is not made up of houses, furniture, land and people. Home is simply thought externalized, and we put into home just what we put into thought, or just what we admit into our individual consciousness; for we must remember that what we express in individual thought, we borrow from either the divine Mind or the carnal mind; and what we bring out in home, business, and life generally, represents what we borrow from the divine Mind or from the carnal mind. A man's business represents his individual mentality and nothing else, and a man's business is governed entirely by what he thinks, and what he thinks represents what he has chosen or selected from either the carnal mind or divine Mind.

Sometimes we are inclined to feel that if our surroundings were different, if we did not have other's thoughts to contend with, or conditions over which we have no apparent control, our lot would not be such a hard one and our problems would be more readily solved. Of course, from a material point of view, that is so; but we are now working things out from another basis, that of Spirit and with a metaphysical understanding of things, and we must face the fact — not one condition of error exists in our business, our home, or our experience, that is not made apparent because of the carnal mind existing in our consciousness.

Don't misunderstand this. I do not mean by this that you and I are responsible for the sin and inharmony which another has made a part of his existence, or for the universal belief that the world is passing through a period of distress. But I do mean that if our consciousness is so permeated with the understanding of the truth of being that we cannot see such conditions as a part of God's creation or existence, they cannot affect or interfere with our demonstrations. Mrs. Eddy says in *Science and Health*, "Jesus beheld in Science the perfect man, who appeared to him where sinning mortal man appears to mortals. In this perfect man the Saviour saw God's own likeness, and this correct view of man healed the sick." Jesus' own consciousness was so filled with the divine that he could not behold a sick man — and because he could not behold a sick man, there was no sick man to heal.

We see, feel, taste, smell, hear and experience just what we hold in consciousness. The same can be said of our homes, our positions, our businesses. Nothing can come into our experience that is not made possible in thought. Our home is an object of our thinking, and therefore we bring out in that home what we think, regardless of what other members of the home may think. We cannot, and we should not want to, control the thinking of others, even those in the home; but if we are conscious of inharmony in our home, it is because of the carnal mind which we entertain in consciousness. We see what we hold in consciousness.

The same in our business. Our business is the manifestation of our own thinking, and no person or condition is really responsible for any experience through which our business passes. You ask, "Am I responsible for the business challenges which have been occurring in the business world the past few years, and for its effects on my business?" No, you might not be personally responsible for them, but you are responsible for the effect on your business. Nothing can come into your business, or your business experiences, which does not come through your own mentality. Nothing can come to your business that your own thinking doesn't make possible. There is nothing to your business but your own thinking, and if you and I were as clear in our thinking about our business as Jesus was about man, nothing but harmony could ever enter our business. So with the understanding that all of our material associations, our material world, our surroundings, our environment, exist only in our thought, we can begin to realize how absolutely you and I have it within our power to regulate and control our own homes and businesses and experiences for good or for bad.

Our world is absolutely individual, our home is individual, our business is individual — all of our own making; and we regulate all of these things for good or for bad in the degree that we admit the carnal or divine to consciousness.

Overcoming Erroneous Conditions

Let us say that in your home there is a condition of inharmony that is seemingly not of your creating. There is a condition or a person there which seems to manifest an erroneous condition for which you are certain you are not responsible. You may not be responsible for the condition; but if you are working in Science, you know that only the carnal mind could be conscious of such a condition; and that if you can remove enough of the carnal from your own thinking by substituting the divine, that condition is bound to be eliminated. Truth is not conscious of error. Only the mortal is conscious of the mortal, and all there is to the mortal is thought. Therefore, if the mortal is completely removed from thought by the influx of the divine, we have no carnal left, and that is treatment, and that is all that treatment is — excluding the carnal from thought by substituting the divine therefor.

So in our home or business, we must know that there is no outside influence responsible for our inharmonies, our mistakes, our failures, and our poverty, etc. All of these things exist in our own thought even though they seem to come to us through persons or conditions over which we have no control. Our right thought about any erroneous condition or person is the truth about that condition or person, and that truth is omnipotent — the only truth. Therefore, by constantly holding the truth in consciousness, the erroneous condition is bound to be eliminated because the erroneous condition is simply thought. We never have a condition of matter to meet. All material conditions are thought; and when a wrong thought is replaced by a right idea, there is but one result — the removal of the wrong thought. We do not have to be concerned as to the time or method of the removal of the error. Our only concern should be to the clarification of our own thought. If we wish to see love in our home, if we wish to see fidelity, obedience, truthfulness, honesty, and purity, we have not only to be loving, faithful, obedient, truthful, honest and pure ourselves, but we have got to so purify our consciousness through the understanding of Truth that we cannot see any of these erroneous qualities as a part of any member of our home. We must see as Jesus saw — "the perfect man."

And the same in our business. We take out of life and out of living what we put into it. If we put in hate, suspicion, faultfinding, fear, worry, dishonesty, unhappiness, and the like, those are the things we will meet up with in our daily contacts, our relations and associations. When we see a dishonest man, we are seeing our own thought. When we see a hateful man, we are seeing our own thought. When we see a poverty-stricken man, we are seeing our own thought. By that I do not mean that we are going to heal everyone we meet of hate or dishonesty, or poverty, but we are going to prevent those people from being channels through which these erroneous conditions can reach us. Someone might be considered as the most dishonest and corrupt person imaginable, but his dishonesty and corruptness could not harm or injure us if our thought about him is clean and Godly. So do you not see how you and I are personally and individually responsible for our own experiences, and how we can individually control and regulate our own experiences for good in the degree that we use the divine in our thinking in place of the carnal?

Joy, real spiritual joy, is one of the most needed qualities today. Joy is the fruit of the Spirit. It is that quality of thought which comes from the understanding of the omnipotence of right thought. The comfort, the security, the supreme and sublime satisfaction and contentment which comes to us as the result of our understanding the effects of right thinking, brings the only true joy there is. There is much more satisfaction and joy in being able to so see our brother man in the light of divine Science, and taking his insult and offense smilingly and lovingly, than there is in getting even with him for his offense. The moment we are consumed with a desire to get even with anyone, just then are we taking into consciousness that much of the carnal which is bound to come back to us one way or another in unpleasant or injurious experiences. With the clear understanding that what we hold in thought we bring into experience, we are very likely to watch our thinking so that we order and regulate our lives so as to bring out a fuller and more complete sense of joy.

We cannot expect to bring out a sense of freedom from sickness, ill-health, disease, and bodily suffering while our consciousness is filled with thoughts of sickness, health-laws, fear of bodily harm, thoughts of hate, anger, malice, or revenge. We cannot bring out harmony in the home and at the same time hold in thought any sense of materiality, differences of opinion, anger, resentment, self-will, self-righteousness, dictation, and so on. We must not only be governed by the divine in our own thinking, but we must watch lest we do not deny others in the home the right to work out their own salvation alone with God. We must not lead. We must be led, and we must recognize the right of others to be led. Human will, domination, or personal dependence will never work out one's problems scientifically. If we are striving to let the divine rule in our individual consciousness, we are not going to go very far wrong in our home and our business associations.

The world in which we live, is but a great picture painted by us individually, and that picture merely represents our individual thoughts. The picture is ugly or beautiful depending on the amount of the carnal or divine painted into it. And remember that we cannot separate the individual thoughts which go to make this picture, so that some of the picture may be beautiful and some ugly. One wrong thought or motive will affect the entire picture. We cannot expect to employ wrong thoughts in our business relations and not have them affect our home relations, and *vice versa*. One wrong motive affects the whole mental canvas. I have seen a man's failing business put on its feet and made successful as a result of a healing in his home relationship. I have see a man's home restored to harmony as a result of a change in his method of thinking in regard to his business. Our thinking constitutes both our home and our business, and we cannot entertain wrong thoughts and motives in connection with one and not have it affect the other. It is like a drop of ink in a tumbler of water. The ink will change the aspect of the whole tumbler of water. And we may be assured and comforted by the conviction that one good thought admitted into consciousness will have its good effect in everything that we undertake. Good thoughts are ideas, and as our world is made up of thought, the more ideas we admit into consciousness the more harmonious will be our entire picture.

We have to think. In fact, all there is to existence is thought, and the more of the divine we allow into consciousness, the more of the divine will appear in the picture which our thoughts create. We cannot entertain divine ideas in thought without bringing into our experience the omnipotence of God; and we do not have to outline, or worry about, or direct as to how these ideas are to work in demonstrations. Demonstration is simply the activity of divine ideas in human consciousness, and the activity of divine ideas in human consciousness is bound to cancel just so much of the carnal in the picture which our thoughts have painted. The activity of divine ideas in human consciousness is what brings health, happiness, prosperity, harmony and the like. Even a grain of Truth held in consciousness will work miracles if we are open and free in thought.

I have a copy of a letter here written by a woman who lived out in one of our western states where they have little rain or water, and at times mere existence is a difficult thing. These people were poor, poverty-stricken, and almost starving because of draught when, through some Christian Science literature which was sent them, consciousness was impregnated with a little glimpse of the divine and a spark of heaven-born hope was kindled in the breasts of these dear people. In explaining their experiences, this lady writes in part as follows:

"The days have been long and sad on Montana's dry prairie this year. Thank you so much for sending the letter and more thanks for sending the good reading stuff you did. Please send me more, as you know we are poor and so is everyone else around here. You know our land is rather low, and consequently we had water and feed after the neighbors had none. Then our slough dried up, and we had to haul water for miles from town. Our horses were poor and weak, and Walter is not much for hard work. He is now past seventy, and it certainly did look dark for us. We had 16 head of cattle, some calves and four horses. They were not anything. We would have given them away if anybody could have given them feed and water. Cattle and horses were lying dead, and the air was foul with the smell of dead animals. The cows had gone dry. We did not get milk or butter. I don't think you can fully understand how hopeless it all was. The $8.00 a month the Government let us have kept us from starving, but not the cattle. Even the Russian Thistle was scarce, but with water we could pull through. I washed dishes once a day in a quart of water and then fed it to the pigs. The chickens were the only things that did well; there were plenty of grasshoppers for them to eat.

"I was hoping and praying that I could die. Then I got this wonderful God-sent literature from you. First, I read the leaflet, 'Divine Love,' then I read the Christian Science lecture. I did not get started on the rest. It seemed as if I was at one with God. I knew then that God had not sent this plague on us; that He loved me and as His child He could help me. It was wonderful! I remembered how God had helped you, and what God had done for you He would do for me.

"That night I dreamed or saw it, I don't know which, but I could see plenty of water coming out of the little gravel hill. I was so sure of it. Walter thought I had gone crazy, but I knew God had told me, and if Moses could get water out of a rock in the wilderness, He surely could give it to us out of a gravel pit. Walter dug and I helped him. At ten feet we got some water, made our curbing and dug on sixteen feet. We got eight feet of water, all we need for ourselves and we are giving some to our neighbors for house use. I am so thankful. I washed clothes every day for six days, and all the dishes are clean. I know it was what we learned about God's love for us in the reading matter you sent that did the work, and please send more."

That is just one illustration of how an inkling of Truth operative in human consciousness will change the entire picture which our wrong thinking has painted. We must constantly hold in thought the truth which we know about God and man, and claim these truths for ourselves, make them a part of our individual consciousness, and they then become a part of the picture which our thoughts have painted as a material world.

I have a copy of a letter purporting to have been written by Mrs. Eddy which is very pertinent here. I doubt very much its authenticity. That is, I doubt that Mrs. Eddy ever wrote it, but it is good and clear and I shall give it here:

"To know that the dragon is in Truth but a mythical creation saves us from it. If we make something of it and attempt to destroy it, we will be vanquished every time. Only TRUTH and LOVE can destroy the dragon.

"What is it to love? To always see the man of God's creation and nothing else and to separate from our thought of men any belief of fear or disease. That is love.

"Let us strive more and more earnestly to reflect this love in our homes where little errors so often tempt us to lose sight of the real child of God.

"We each dwell in our own world of consciousness. We look out through the windows of this consciousness, and behold the passing procession of mortal mind.

"Day after day we have been lured forth — been pressed into the whirl, lost our individual peace and poise in divine Mind and found ourselves dragged through the weariness, the uncleanness and pain of the procession.

"We seek to regain our own home of consciousness, wiser for the experience — thinking we will not again become a part of error's pageant, but here let the understanding of love guard well your door. Stay in your own house of demonstration. Keep your peace, for idle curiosity, criticism, or even false sympathy may lure you forth. Wherein lies the wisdom of the serpent? To hide itself. Therefore hide yourself in the understanding of Christian Science.

"Be it small or great we have all needed the experiences we have had. Never be found, as a Christian Scientist, mourning over any experience. It is a thing of the past, but not so the manifold power and presence of God resulting therefrom."

Remember that all being is consciousness, and that the consciousness you entertain of dominion and abundance, through reflection, determines the outward in your experience. All of the ideas of Mind constitute man — hence man has dominion and abundance. This consciousness of abundance cancels in our consciousness the argument of lack; and when the argument of lack is removed from our consciousness, it is removed from the picture which our thinking creates. So do you not see that we do not have to work for supply or health or relationships? The consciousness which knows no lack is bound to be conscious of abundance. That consciousness which recognizes no sickness is bound to be conscious of health.

We pick our mortal thoughts out of mortal mind which claims to exist as one mind outside our individual consciousness, and to the extent that we admit these carnal thoughts into consciousness is our world material. We do not see a material world. We see our own thoughts — that is, we see those thoughts which we have admitted to consciousness from the carnal mind. To the extent that we admit these thoughts to consciousness are we subjecting ourselves to the laws of mortal mind, which laws may operate to our injury and detriment, even though we may not be conscious of the existence of those laws.

The Book of Job is a most excellent portrayal of the arguments of animal magnetism which come to each and everyone of us for acceptance or rejection. The various characters portrayed in this Book and the arguments which they presented to Job, signify the varying phases of animal magnetism which present themselves to each and everyone of us in our everyday lives. These arguments, as we see here, even come to us in the guise of good times, and unless we are alert and are able to weigh these arguments and determine from our understanding and the standpoint of spirituality whence they come and where they will lead us if listened to, we are likely to get into the same mental state as that in which Job found himself.

We find in the first place, Job as a prosperous, God-fearing man, with money, possessions, standing in the community, honored, looked up to, admired, with a good-sized family and with everything in the world one could wish for from a material standpoint. Then, as Job is contemplating on all these things, and perhaps doing his mental work in what he thought was a good and righteous manner, there comes the lurking and subtle suggestion that perhaps he is some great man and that he himself had accomplished all of these wonderful things. This was the Devil coming along with the Lord to communicate with Job. The Devil suggested to Job that maybe he had had a greater hand in all of this getting of good than God had, and because of this, the Devil (the mental argument) says,

"Suppose all of these good things were taken away from you, then how long would you love the Lord? Let's see which is the stronger? Your faith in God or your faith in your own human ability? Let us see just how great a man you are with all your possessions and human ability." And eventually everything that Job had gained was swept away from him. Why? Because he believed within himself that he was some great person, separate and apart from God. His own thoughts as to how all of these things came to him were his own undoing. Nothing will bring our downfall quicker than egotism, and nothing will keep us down longer. One must have confidence in himself as a child of God, as the reflection of all the intelligence, wisdom, humility and ability there is, but he must not let the shadow of his own importance, intelligence, and past achievements blind him to the fact that he of himself can do nothing.

Read this Book of Job often. It will do you much good, if you read it with an understanding heart and with a humble desire to learn how to proceed to that success which knows no failure. Try to get the lesson there for you. Don't try to figure out how this applies to someone else. You are the one who needs saving, and the lesson in this Book that is there for you is the lesson you are after.

If things are not going well with you, with your business, or your home; if there does not seem to be a constant and steady improvement in all of your affairs; if you feel that you are in a rut, that your Science is not working out things for you as it should; if you are inclined to neglect your mental work and your reading; if your interest in Science lags at times, and you do not seem to see any results, what is the answer? You need to read the Book of Job, or something that will stir you to a new base of thought. You need to change your thinking. And that is the only thing in the world you do need to change. You need to pray, and pray hard and long. You need to immerse yourself in the great heart of God by a constant and selfless communion with Him in prayer. Your salvation, business, home affairs, environment, all exist in your own consciousness, and you can only change the outward manifestation of things by changing your inward convictions.

If things aren't well with you, you are thinking wrongly, and I don't know anything easier in this world to do than to change one's thinking. If you can change from a state of failure to a state of abundance and success by a change of thought, why not change? Often the most egotistical man recognizes his own shortcomings the least. A man's egotism, arrogance, self-opinion and pride of accomplishment will do more to wreck his career than anything I know. A self-opinionated, arrogant, egotistical man is an offense not only to God, but to his brother man; and he will find it hard to keep close contact with either. The humblest man has the most friends and obtains the most favors from God.

If you will take up once in a while a study of Job with the understanding that all of his misfortunes were self-inflicted, even though he had been a good, upright, devout man, you may get something that will turn the tide in the affairs of your entire life. We all carve out our own fortunes or destinies just as sure as there is a God; and, as I have said, if things are not going right with us, it is because of our own individual thinking and not because of our environment, our surroundings, or the activities or misfortunes of others. For instance, as an example of how one's self-righteousness will try to argue that he is being sadly and badly abused and mistreated because of all these misfortunes which have come upon him, we find Eliphaz, the Temanite, arguing with Job. Now Eliphaz simply represents a quality of thought, possibly self-righteousness or self-pity. Eliphaz, or self-pity, says to Job, "Behold thou hast instructed many, and thou hast strengthened the weak hands. Thy words have upholden him that was falling, and thou hast strengthened the feeble knees. But now it comes upon thee and thou faintest. It toucheth thee and thou art troubled."

And so on through the entire Book of Job. There we find the arguments of the carnal mind which present themselves to us in a thousand different ways. And as long as Job was willing to argue with these thoughts of animal magnetism, just so long was he troubled. But just as soon as he threw off these arguments of the carnal, just as soon as he was willing to listen to no one but God and stop arguing pro and con, he came into his own. And so it is with everyone of us. We must stop our arguments with mortal mind. Instead of arguing with them, we must put them out of consciousness, and the very fact that we can put them out of consciousness is proof that they not only come to us from without, but that they have no real origin or existence. If they were real and came from Mind, they could not be put out.

Stick to your understanding of God. Never waiver. Never doubt. He will care for you as He does for the lilies, and though at times the clouds may seem dark, if you are faithful in your allegiance to Him, you will come forth with colors flying and with hearts rejoicing.

OUR RIGHT TO TRUE INDIVIDUALISM

Association Address of 1934

Christian Scientists should learn to think and to think for themselves, unaided and unhindered by any of the arguments of others, including aggressive mental suggestion from without. What a boon it is to have with us always that which we know is true and right, and whereby we can weigh all thoughts and thus determine their source and ultimate. We may often determine the source of a thought by determining its ultimate. But always try and think for yourselves, and let your judgment, reasoning, and deductions be based on your understanding of God and man, and not on personal opinions, likes, dislikes, political tendencies, breeding or inclinations. Be a child of God and not a child of man. Be independent and you will be free. Be individualistic and you will not be muddled or confused by high-sounding phrases, schemes or plans.

The Synonyms

What is God? What is man? God is *Mind.* Mind is reflected how? By spiritual intelligence. Spiritual intelligence, then, constitutes man. Spiritual intelligence is expressed through you and me right here and now in our thinking. And that intelligence comes from the only Mind there is. In fact, that intelligence *is* that Mind. That Mind is omnipotent. Therefore, when you and I are expressing spiritual intelligence, we are expressing omnipotence. Always bear that in mind. Your right thinking is omnipotence with you. The reason we are not bringing out the fruits of the Spirit is because we are not thinking with that conviction borne of understanding. We still, I am afraid, look upon our God as something afar off, even when we think of Him as Mind. We do not seem to have arrived yet at the point where we are willing to endow our right thinking with the sense or understanding of omnipotence which is God. Spiritual thinking, or right thinking, is God with us. It is not a reflection of a Mind which is separated from us. It is God with us, and God with us is omnipotence with us. Spiritual intelligence is the presence of spiritual ideas in consciousness, and an idea comes from God. These ideas existing in our consciousness constitute our sonship with God, and as the Father and the Son are one, then we have with us the omnipotence of the one God when we are thinking rightly.

A divine idea in consciousness is in itself omnipotence. We do not have to endow a divine idea with omnipotence. The very presence in thought of those ideas constitutes omnipotence, and this omnipotence, if left alone, without the intervention of our own doubts and fears, will work the works of omnipotence. A right idea is omnipotent in and of itself, and the presence of a right idea in our consciousness is all that you and I are concerned about. The omnipotence is taken care of by God, and the work is done by Him. Our obligation, as far as a particular idea is concerned, ceases with the presence of that idea in thought. If we will let God do the work, He will do it.

God is *Spirit*, which means that all of God's ideas are ever present awaiting admission into consciousness. We do not have to search for God's ideas. We certainly do not have to manufacture them. They are here and now existing in infinity, surrounding us, encompassing us and awaiting admission to our consciousness. As St. Paul puts it, "In Him we live and move and have our being." All that you and I have to do is to realize the ever presence of these ideas and open our consciousness to them, let them in, and we have then allied ourselves to the omnipotence of God. The realization of this ever presence of His ideas brings out to our consciousness the sense of God as Spirit ever present.

God is *Truth*, and what has been said of Spirit and ideas of Mind may be said of Truth. Truth is Spirit because both are God.

Therefore Truth is ever present; and as there is but one Truth about anything and everything, and one Mind, there can be no confusion and no opposite of Truth. If Truth has no opposite (and it cannot have an opposite if there is but one God), then nothing can come into the experience of man which can make a lie, argue for confusion of thought, inharmony, discouragement or indecision.

Truth must be the opposite of error; and as God is Truth and Truth fills all space, there can be no error. The sense that there is no opposite of God as error, brings out the true sense of God as Truth. And this sense of Truth, or ideas, in consciousness brings out again the true sense of omnipotence in our right thinking. We must be so certain of the omnipotence of our right thinking that any sense of doubt or anxiety or fear will be foreign to our experience. We cannot doubt, we cannot fear, we cannot be anxious or undecided, if we are realizing the omnipotence, the omniscience and the omnipresence of God. This consciousness of God, or this divine consciousness, brings out to us the sense of God as *Soul*. The Soul of man is God in consciousness. The Soul of man is divine consciousness. The Soul of man is the Christ, the Holy Ghost, the man of God's creating.

As we know, the Christ is Truth made manifest in human consciousness. Mrs. Eddy uses the word Christ and the term Truth synonymously, apparently; and as the Father and the Son are one, there is, in reality, only the distinction between the two, of application. The Christ, then, is Truth made manifest to human consciousness. This Christ, this Truth made manifest to human consciousness, is omnipotence. The only difference between the Christ and the Truth is one of application or consciousness. When Truth becomes operative in human consciousness, it is the Christ, or the Saviour. This Christ, this Truth, operative in human consciousness naturally rules out of consciousness that which is its supposed opposite.

The supposed opposite of Truth is, of course, carnality, hate, belief in matter and evil. When these beliefs of matter, evil, death, are ruled out of thought, what is left? Eternity, harmony, peace, love. And eternity is expressed in *Life*. God must be Life if the understanding of God in consciousness does away with that which leads to death — such as sickness, matter, evil. So God must be Life. The understanding of this in our individual consciousness, the understanding that our right thinking, our pure thinking, our spiritual thinking, is Life, must result in length of days far beyond the three score years and ten supposedly allotted to man. Should not Christian Scientists right now be demonstrating length of days, vigor, freshness, youth?

One of the things I want to stress is the necessity of bringing out length of days, not theoretically, but practically. The true sense of God as Life, and the understanding of the omnipotence of this sense in our thinking, will bring out the true sense of Life which knows no sickness, decrepitude, senility or death. We must recognize that the God-consciousness has no opposing elements, no conflicting thought, no hindrance; that God is *Principle*, the originator and the conclusion of all things, the Alpha and Omega of existence, the beginning and the ending. Truth is eternal. It always has been and always will be. It never changes; it never has changed. It recognizes existence as complete, without beginning and without end. Thus there is no formative process to existence. It is, in its entirety, here and now. That realization brings out Principle, law. No beginning, no ending, no formation — just unfoldment. Everything is; God is the Alpha and Omega. And that is Principle.

It is a wonderful thought — this thought of God as Principle. It relieves us of the necessity of bringing something to pass, of accomplishing a healing or of changing anything but thought. Everything is complete here and now, and our change of thought to encompass this great verity of being and existence will lead us into the realm of the infinite, into the paths of limitless possibilities and accomplishment. Dwell on God as Principle often and long. It will enlarge your vision, broaden your aspirations, and assure your accomplishments.

And need we say aught of *Love*, the keynote of all true understanding of God? Without a true concept of God as Love, what would God as Mind, Truth, Soul, Spirit, Principle and Life amount to? Nothing. "Though I have all of these things and have not charity [Love] I am as sounding brass and a tinkling cymbal." Love makes many demands on our understanding of and devotion to Principle, and how far short of the divine requirements we have fallen may be determined in our lack of demonstration. We may understand God as Mind, Principle, Soul, Spirit, Life, Truth; but with all of this, unless we can understand Him as Love, and express that Love in our thinking, our work is fruitless.

That God is Life, Truth, Spirit, Soul, Mind and Principle, might be said to express the *letter* of Christianity, but God as Love might be said to express the *spirit* of Christianity. Understanding without Love becomes pedantic, pulseless and soulless. Love is impersonal. Mrs. Eddy was asked how one was to love in a divine way. She replied, "Love not persons or things, just love."

If our mind is filled with love, we are not hating anyone or anything. Love is that which, when held in consciousness, prevents us from seeing our brother man in any light but spiritual. Love is that which prevents us from seeing our brother man as dishonest, untruthful, sinful, weak, poverty-stricken, or sick. We can arrive at that point in our understanding of God and man where we can see our brother man as Mrs. Eddy tells us Jesus saw him: "Jesus beheld in Science the perfect man, who appeared to him where sinning mortal man appears to mortals. In this perfect man the Saviour saw God's own likeness, and this correct view of man healed the sick." When we arrive at that point in our understanding of God and man where our view of our brother man heals him instantaneously of sickness and of sin, then we will have accomplished something in the direction of perceiving God as Love. It is our perception of God as Love and our willingness to be governed by Love, more than our perception of God as Mind, Life, Truth, Spirit, Soul and Principle, which heals the sick.

In *Science and Health* Mrs. Eddy has written: "Comeliness and grace are independent of matter. Being possesses its qualities before they are perceived humanly. Beauty is a thing of Life, which dwells forever in the eternal Mind and reflects the charms of His goodness in expression, form, outline, and color. It is Love which paints the petal with myriad hues, glances in the warm sunbeam, arches the cloud with the bow of beauty, blazons the night with starry gems, and covers earth with loveliness."

Human Consciousness

This quotation brings us into the further question of the "human consciousness" and the admission of divine ideas into this consciousness. In her writings Mrs. Eddy, as we know, uses "human mind" and "mortal mind" interchangeably in some instances, but throughout her writings she makes a decided distinction between the "human consciousness" and "mortal consciousness," and a careful study of her writings reveals a constant and continuous differentiation between "human mind" and "mortal mind" or "carnal mind."

In *Science and Health* Mrs. Eddy says, "If mortal mind knew how to be better, it would be better." It is obvious that that which is mortal could not even be conscious of that which is immortal. Evil could never be conscious of good. It would be impossible for evil to know good, because there is nothing in evil to enable it to recognize good. The only explanation of evil is the "absence of good." *Evil is the absence of good.* So we can never hope to improve mortal mind. But something must be improved to provide a method of escape from mortality and mortal living, with its accompanying ills of sickness and poverty and discord. There must be some process of progression out of evil into good. There must be a state of consciousness where the exchange from evil to good can be made.

Now, evil has only the power or reality given it in individual belief. Therefore, the process of progression from evil to good is not one of change. It is not changing evil into good. It is changing thought wherein the good *replaces* the evil. This change is made in what Mrs. Eddy has termed the *human consciousness*. The evil in human consciousness is not cognizant of the good in human consciousness. They are as distinct and separate as the two poles, because evil does not exist except in belief, while good exists in truth and reality. The truth we entertain in consciousness exists as conviction; the evil we entertain exists as belief or illusion. That state of existence which entertains truth as a conviction and error as an illusion is called by Mrs. Eddy the human consciousness.

Now, human consciousness is neither person, place nor thing. It is just consciousness. Because this consciousness has taken unto itself certain beliefs of mortal mind such as personal sense, evil, materiality, matter, it has embodied itself in that which you and I call a human body. Besides this material embodiment, this state of consciousness includes some little gleam of goodness and spirituality which in themselves are not conscious of this claim of human embodiment. The claim of human embodiment is mortal mind which is conscious only of itself. So the human consciousness does not create the material body and the material world; it is the carnal mind admitted to and held in human consciousness which constitutes the human body and material existence.

In the Preface to *Science and Health* Mrs. Eddy writes: "The physical healing of Christian Science results now, as in Jesus' time, from the operation of divine Principle, before which sin and disease lose their reality in human consciousness and disappear as naturally and as necessarily as darkness gives place to light and sin to reformation."

In other passages she says: "Material sense does not unfold the facts of existence; but spiritual sense lifts human consciousness into eternal Truth." "Christ is the true idea voicing good, the divine message from God to man speaking to the human consciousness." " . . . the heavens and earth to one human consciousness, that consciousness which God bestows, are spiritual, while to another, the unillumined human mind, the vision is material." "The human mind acts more powerfully to offset the discords of matter and the ills of flesh, in proportion as it puts less weight into the material or fleshly scale and more weight into the spiritual scale."

Mrs. Eddy also brings out very distinctly the different parts played in human existence by the human mind, the mortal mind and the divine Mind. She there says: "If it were not what the human mind says of the body, the body, like the inanimate wheel, would never be weary. What renders both sin and sickness difficult of cure is, that the human mind is the sinner, disinclined to self correction, and believing that the body can be sick independently of mortal mind and that the divine Mind has no jurisdiction over the body."

All of these quotations I shall analyze further on. Again she makes the same distinction between the human, the mortal, and the divine where she says: "We must learn how mankind govern the body — whether through faith in hygiene, in drugs, and in will-power. We should learn whether they govern the body through a belief in the necessity of sickness and death, sin and pardon, or govern it from the higher understanding that the divine Mind makes perfect, acts upon the so-called human mind through Truth, leads the human mind to relinquish all error, to find the divine Mind to be the only Mind, and the healer of sin, disease and death." (Marginal Heading, "Mortal mind's disappearance") And she also says that "the human mind alone suffers."

With all of these quotations in mind, I want to return to the one that says, "Comeliness and grace are independent of matter. Being possesses its qualities before they are perceived humanly." Here is a clear statement that God and His creation exist separate and distinct from human consciousness. Mrs. Eddy here recognizes a state of consciousness which she calls human and in which the divine has not made any appearance or impression — in which, in other words, the divine does not exist. The human is just a state of individualized consciousness, an error of belief, because, she says, "Being possesses its qualities before they are perceived humanly."

So it is possible to conceive of a human consciousness devoid of an understanding of the realities of being. When this human consciousness, through the process of thought, begins to take on some of the qualities of being or of God, it then begins to take on divine hues and become evangelized. This consciousness would not, of course, need evangelization if it were true consciousness, or the consciousness of God — in other words, if it were that consciousness which constitutes the true man, or real man of God's creating. The human consciousness might be said to be the belief in a consciousness separate and distinct from God — just a belief of consciousness without being good or bad. This consciousness is capable of accepting good or evil according to human belief. As this consciousness begins to take unto itself mortal mind, it begins to call itself mortal man. The claim of a consciousness separate and apart from God exists in its primitive state without the consciousness of evil. Our Leader writes in *Unity of Good*: "The more I understand true humanhood, the more I see it to be sinless."

The human begins to take on some of the carnal mind, and this carnal mind is what gives to the human consciousness a belief of a material or physical body, the belief of birth, growth, maturity, death; the belief of sickness, sin, unhappiness, misery, inharmony, discord. The body of mortal mind in its primitive state is a perfect human concept, a body free from sickness, poverty, sin. In other words, mortal mind's idea is a material body free from sickness or any of the accompanying or secondary beliefs of the carnal mind.

The human consciousness then may be said to take to itself first the belief of a human body without any of the beliefs of sickness or inharmony. Then the human consciousness takes to itself a little more of the carnal mind, and this carnal mind admitted to human consciousness is expressed in a sick mortal body, a sinful mortal body, a poverty-stricken mortal body.

That which becomes an object of human consciousness as matter, sin, sickness, and poverty, must have first existed in the carnal mind outside human consciousness. That is, the human consciousness could not be conscious of a mortal body without first admitting mortal mind. This mortal mind admitted to human consciousness is, in turn, objectified or projected as matter, or belief of matter. The mortal mind does not become material until it enters human consciousness and is in turn projected.

There are three states or stages of supposed existence of matter and the material: the *first footstep*, the carnal or mortal mind claiming existence as one mind outside of human consciousness. The carnal or mortal mind existing as a false belief outside human consciousness is not material and has no material accompaniments or elements, as you and I view materiality. The carnal mind is admitted to human consciousness without any sense of materiality and does not assume material proportions until its projection or objectification. So the *second footstep* in individual carnal or material existence, is the acceptance into human consciousness of this carnal mind. The *third footstep* in the process, is the objectification of the carnal in thought as matter. So matter becomes an object of individual thought, and the only way whereby the human consciousness will ever be able to rid itself of matter is through the de-materialization of thought.

And so do you not see how thoroughly individual human existence is? Do you not see how you and I make our own worlds of matter by our own thinking, and how individual must be our process and method of salvation from matter? You and I create our own consciousness, for these determine our individual material existence, and our individual worlds. No one else can do our thinking for us. Therefore no thoughts but our own create our individual worlds, and it depends on our thinking just what kind of thoughts we admit into consciousness, for these determine our individual material existence,and so no thoughts but our own can free us from the bondage of the carnal mind. We admit the carnal into thought.

And how are we to put these thoughts out of consciousness? Why, by exchanging for them divine ideas. It is a process of replacement. Now, if the carnal or the material can be done away with by thought, then that is proof enough that the material has neither life, truth, intelligence nor substance. If, by replacing the carnal with the divine, we can rid ourselves of matter, then we have proven that not only matter is unreal, but also the thought which creates matter is unreal. Thus we arrive at the conclusion that material existence is an illusion. It is an illusion of what? Of the carnal mind. Whence comes the carnal mind? It never came. It is *not* because God did not create it. Therefore, material existence is in reality not an existence of the carnal mind or carnal existence; it is rather *the absence of the divine*, and as the divine is the only Mind there is, and as material existence is a suppositious state of a mind which does not exist, there is in reality no material existence to be saved from.

Material existence is a state of unconsciousness, because it is the supposed absence of the only Mind there is. It is not a creation of the carnal mind. It is, rather, the supposed absence of the divine. So salvation from materiality, or unconsciousness, does not involve putting off the carnal so much as it does putting on the spiritual. Putting on the spiritual — that is, thinking divine ideas — is simply a state of awakening from our state of unconsciousness into our true state of spiritual existence. So thus do we realize the necessity of devoting time and thought to the spiritual, rather than to overcoming that which does not, in reality, exist. So material existence is strictly individual, and salvation from material existence is strictly individual. No one has made the carnal world for you, and no one can pray, push, pull or pardon you into the kingdom of heaven. Everything is individual.

Because material creation is individual, salvation must be individual. The material does not exist outside of your and my thinking. Creation is individual, and outside of your and my consciousness, matter does not exist. Matter only exists in thought. Each individual human consciousness has created its own material world with the use of the carnal mind which it has admitted. The human consciousness creates matter with the aid of the carnal mind, and each individual object of material creation is strictly individual even though there are many human consciousnesses to be conscious of such creation.

Our Individual Consciousness Creates Our World

There are as many worlds and as many material objects of creation as there are individuals. For instance, a short time ago I cut the following from the column of O. O. McIntyre, the noted columnist and syndicate writer: "I sat listening the other evening to a group of professional gentlemen mooting the prolegomena (preliminary considerations) of science. To them, it was debatable whether the table at which they grouped could be said to really exist when there's nobody to see it. In their reasoning it was merely a whirl of molecules. A mental projection. All very interesting but highly confusing, for it does not seem so many men could be sitting around kidding themselves. Any way, I left fluttering with the ork-orks."

Thus we see that physical scientists are beginning to glimpse in a small way what Mrs. Eddy gave to the world when she wrote *Science and Health*. We not only create our own material worlds individually, but we endow that material world with just exactly what exists in our own consciousness. We each, individually, endow our world with sickness, sorrow, dishonesty, injustice, poverty, and the like. If we did not, where would come any hope of relief or salvation? If dishonesty, sickness, poverty, and sin, which exists in our individual worlds, both in ourselves and in others, were not the objects of our own individual states of consciousness, wherein would be found any relief from these ills?

We cannot prevent others from thinking just as they wish to think, and therefore we cannot prevent others from thinking in a dishonest or sinful manner. If we had to wait for God to heal another of his dishonesty before we could have a world free from dishonesty, there would be little hope for ultimate individual salvation. If we had to wait for the whole world to be saved from the carnal mind, then there would be little incentive for personal and individual endeavor; but when we realize that our world is an individual world of our own individual creating, and that all that exists in that world exists there because of our own thinking — that our world is simply our own state of consciousness — then we can begin right now to change our entire material outlook by changing our own individual thinking.

If we could see man so clearly as a child of God, free from sin, sickness, dishonesty, and the like, then we would never see a dishonest man, a sick man, a sinful man, or a poverty-stricken man. All that we are conscious of in our material world exists in our own thinking, so do you not see how thoroughly individual our work and salvation must be? No one in the world can think for you and me. Therefore no one in the world can take away from our material world any of the sin, the sickness and the misery of it. We must do that ourselves by our own purification of thought — by exchanging in our own thinking the divine for the carnal. This is so clearly brought out in the first few verses of the Second Chapter of Romans where it is written: "Therefore thou art inexcusable, O man, whosoever thou art that judgest; for wherein thou judgest another, thou condemnest thyself: for thou that judgest doeth the same things."

It behooves us not to attempt to sit in judgment on the shortcomings of our brother man because we would not be conscious of the wrong of our neighbor except for the evil in our own consciousness. So when we are tempted to believe that someone is trying to do us an injury, is acting unjustly towards us, is dishonest, hateful, revengeful, or that we are the object of the malicious mental malpractice of another, what is our remedy? Is it to treat the channel through which we believe all of these evils are manifesting themselves? *No!* It is to treat ourselves, to purify our own thinking, so that we can see our brother man as a child of God, pure and free from all of these claims which the mortal mind in our own consciousness makes us believe belongs to another. This is the Science of Christianity. This is true Christian Science.

We must understand that all that exists in our material world was manufactured in our own consciousness with the carnal mind as the material with which we do our manufacturing. The carnal mind has no existence and no object or subject until we give it place in belief or consciousness. To go back then to the passage from *Science and Health*, "Being [that is, God and His creation] possesses its qualities before they are perceived humanly."

Love Essential to Progress

When the qualities of Mind are humanly perceived and held in consciousness, then existence begins to assume divine proportions. Our material world is simply the carnal in our own individual thinking objectified. Then, when we begin to take into consciousness some of the divine, those divine ideas are likewise projected, not as matter, but to the extent of canceling that much of matter in the mortal picture which the carnal mind has drawn for us as matter.

We have a world, we will say, of matter in which there is hate and all that goes to make up material existence. Now, this hate exists in that world only because of our thinking. Now, we begin to take into consciousness a little sense of divine Love. We begin, we will say, to become conscious of God as Love. This understanding of God as Love dwelling in our consciousness, is bound to take place in our conscious existence, and that hate which this Love has displaced ceases to be a part of our conscious existence. Thus does our material picture improve with the influx of the divine into consciousness until sooner or later there has come enough of the divine into thought to replace all of the carnal and then existence becomes spiritual — wholly spiritual — and the millennium will have been reached. In this same passage from *Science and Health*, Mrs. Eddy has written: "It is Love which paints the petal with myriad hues, glances in the warm sunbeam, arches the cloud with the bow of beauty, blazons the night with starry gems and covers the earth with loveliness."

To accomplish all of this, where must this Love exist but in human consciousness? It is the divine in a human consciousness which makes all things new and brings beauty, sublimity, sweetness, joy, harmony and peace into individual, material existence. Love has no power to enrich your and my existence until it dwells in our individual consciousness to the exclusion of that which claims to be its opposite. Love does not come down from above and panoply you and me with its beneficent influence. Love must be admitted into consciousness and retained there in order that the petal may be painted with myriad hues and that the earth may be covered with loveliness. And how essential it is to know and appreciate what Love really is! Love, unexpressed, is not love.

Man, we learn in Christian Science, is God reflected. God is Love. Therefore, Love reflected is man. Love unreflected is not man. Therefore, just to believe that God is Love and that man is the image and likeness of God, is not enough. It is not enough for man, and it is not enough for God. Hence, to become men of God and bring ourselves under God's laws of health, happiness, harmony, abundance, we must reflect Love. No one is more miserable or more devoid of the presence of God and His infinite goodness than the man or woman who does not understand how to express love. And in this connection, one must constantly work to know that he cannot be governed by family influences, traits, characteristics or tendencies. And he must constantly know that no influence of national characteristics can govern man. I know from bitter experience what it is to be held in bondage to the belief that one must not evidence enthusiasm, love, joy, and so on.

Nothing will hinder one's growth so much as the suppression of love and loving sentiments, and nothing will aid in that suppression so much as harboring the belief of family traits, characteristics, or influence. Don't be afraid that you are going farther than the other fellow in your expressions of love and gratitude and appreciation. Don't hold to the fifty-fifty idea in your relations with men. All you are concerned about is your own growth and your own ability to demonstrate freedom from material bondage to the extent that you can express health, happiness and abundance. You are not concerned in what the other fellow may do or feel.

Someone else, some member of the family, may not understand about Christian Science; or, understanding about it, he does not seem able to demonstrate it to the full extent of expressing love and kindness and consideration around the house. Your remedy does not lie in meeting that thought halfway, and only going as far as he or she goes. Your remedy lies in your demonstration of God to the extent that you can express the true man. You cannot express true manhood and true womanhood if you are going to let the demonstration of another be your measuring rod of endeavor. Your expressions of love and gratitude and freedom measure your manhood or womanhood, and because another falls short, you certainly are not going to cheat yourself by curtailing your sonship with God because someone else has not been able to demonstrate the light.

In certain nationalities, the expression of loving, charitable and forgiving sentiment is almost an impossibility. This you must work against. Some families just naturally do not find it possible to express lovingkindness, charitableness, freedom and ease with others, although inwardly they feel the urge to do so. Some seem to think they cannot express their feelings; some seem to think they should not express their feelings; and they go through life more or less isolated, shut in, cold, miserable and seemingly heartless. Such are to be pitied and loved and helped. Nothing is more discouraging and stultifying than to feel sentiments which one is unable to express. We must learn that man is God expressed, and we understand that lofty, high-loving and even sentimental sentiments unexpressed, separate us from God and tend to fasten on us the mortal arguments of sickness, unhappiness and poverty. Then we begin to see the necessity of loosening up as it were, and of giving free vent to our feelings, even though these sentiments expressed may not be exactly understood or even appreciated by those about us.

We are, too often, governed in our activities, and even our thoughts, by the fear of what others may think, or by the fear that our sentiments or activities will not be appreciated, and thus we question the advisability of expressing them. What someone else may think, and how others may take our exhibitions of love and gratitude and spontaneity, is not the point with us. The point is, are we expressing true manhood and womanhood? Are we reflecting God? If we are, then we are allying ourselves with God, and availing ourselves of His blessings. If we are not expressing or reflecting our true selfhood with the Father, simply because we are wondering what someone else may think, or whether our good efforts will be lost on the desert air, then we are willfully denying ourselves that which this true reflection is bound to bring to us.

I am inclined to dwell, perhaps, a little too long on this point because I have been so intimately associated with conditions which come under the above descriptions. I know how barren a life can be under the condition of suppression. I know how utterly miserable and useless one may become because of the fear of another's opinion. I know how the bonds of inherited conservatism and family characteristics and influences can strangle and stultify. And so I urge you to watch these traits of character which sap the very foundations of true existence and lead us into barren and fruitless lives. Don't be manlike. Be God-like, and you will never lose. Loosen up. Don't be afraid to express more love and affection and consideration about the house. No one is going to think you are weak or entering your second childhood. More than likely you are going to put a little secret joy and warmth into some longing soul. A kind word, an appreciative word, a touch, a caress, an interest in the welfare and efforts of another will not rob you. They will, rather, enrich you beyond the power of contemplation. In the words of our Master given to us in the Sermon on the Mount: "Ye are the salt of the earth: but if the salt have lost its savor, wherewith shall it be salted? It is thenceforth good for nothing, but to be cast out, and to be trodden under the foot of men. Ye are the light of the world. A city that is set on a hill cannot be hid. Neither do men light a candle, and put it under a bushel, but on a candlestick; and it giveth light unto all that are in the house. Let your light so shine before men, that they may see your good works, and glorify your Father which is in heaven." In other words, love that is unexpressed (hidden under a bushel) is not love, and therefore is not man.

Origin of Carnal Thoughts

Remember that carnal thoughts do not originate in brain. I have been questioned on several occasions as to the correctness of this from the standpoint of Christian Science, but nevertheless the statement stands. I want you to be clear on this: that a carnal thought never was created by a mortal or originated in a brain. A carnal thought comes from that one mortal mind which exists outside of mortal man. Mortal mind claims to be one just as divine Mind is one. In *Retrospection and Introspection*, Mrs. Eddy says: "The sin is the sinner, and *vice versa*, for such is the unity of evil; and together both sinner and sin will be destroyed by the supremacy of good. This, however, does not annihilate man, for to efface sin, alias the sinner, brings to light, makes apparent, the real man, even God's 'image and likeness.' Need it be said that any opposite theory is heterodox to divine Science, which teaches that good is equally one and all, even as the opposite claim of evil is one."

So the carnal mind and all that comes from it is one, and comes from without mortal man. If it originated in the brain, where would there be any hope for relief or freedom? If the brain, independent of mortal mind, originated an evil thought, we would be helpless victims of that thought and could never free ourselves from it. We would be helpless sinners and sufferers. We have no control over the brain from the theory of mortal existence, but seem to be victims of the brain. If, then, the brain created thought, how and by what means could you and I overcome or control thought? We could not. In *Science and Health* Mrs. Eddy says, "Remember, brain is not mind." And she also says that "brain-lobes cannot think."

In *Retrospection and Introspection* Mrs. Eddy says, "Sin,"

that is, the carnal mind, "existed as a false claim before the human concept of sin was formed;" that is, the carnal mind exists outside human consciousness, and it is only when human consciousness admits the carnal mind that the human concept of sin is formed. Now the human concept of sin is matter and the material universe, with its sin, sickness, poverty and death. So here we have as clear a statement as one could find to the effect that the carnal mind and the human consciousness are separate and distinct states of error. Sin, she says here, exists aside and distinct from human consciousness — your and my consciousness. When sin, or the carnal mind, is admitted to human consciousness, then that carnal mind is in turn objectified as "the human concept," or matter.

In this same article, in further proof that the carnal exists outside human consciousness, Mrs. Eddy goes on to say, "Hence, one's concept of error is not the whole of error." That is, one's concept of error consists only of that which one admits into consciousness and no more. So each individual concept of existence consists only of what one admits into consciousness. It is evident that each one of us admits different quantities of the carnal into consciousness and that no one consciousness holds all of the carnal mind. Therefore, as Mrs. Eddy says, " . . . one's concept of error is not all of error." Her further statement in this article on "The Human Concept," that "sin is both concrete and abstract," is only additional proof that the carnal mind becomes materialized only as it becomes active in individual human consciousness. The carnal mind exists in its abstract state (that is, without any physical evidence or tangibility) outside human consciousness; but just as soon as it is admitted to and becomes a part of the human consciousness, it becomes concrete. That is, it has evidence. It becomes material. It becomes tangible to human consciousness. I am dwelling on this because it is an important point in the understanding of human existence, and to your practice in Christian Science.

Take the passage from *Science and Health*, quoted above, where Mrs. Eddy says, "The human mind acts more powerfully to offset the discords of matter and the ills of the flesh, in proportion as it [the human mind] puts less weight into the material or fleshly scale [that is, the carnal], and more weight into the spiritual scale." Here is a direct recognition or statement regarding the three states of consciousness. She plainly says that the human mind puts less weight in the carnal mind and more weight in the divine Mind. And again in *Science and Health* Mrs. Eddy says, "The heavens and earth to one human consciousness, that consciousness which God bestows [that is, that consciousness which is animated solely by the divine Mind] are spiritual, while to another, the unillumined human mind [that is, that mind which has not been imbued with the spiritual and is wholly carnal], the vision is material." The textbook also states: "We must learn how mankind govern the body. . . . We should learn whether they govern the body through a belief in the necessity of sickness and death, sin and pardon, or govern it from the higher understanding that the divine Mind makes perfect, acts upon the so-called human mind through truth, leads the human mind to relinquish all error [that is, the carnal mind], to find the divine Mind to be the only Mind, and the healer of sin, disease and death." The marginal note to this paragraph reads, "Mortal mind's disappearance." You will note that mortal mind is not changed. It disappears. It is replaced in the human consciousness by the divine Mind.

In this connection, I call your attention to the "trial" in *Science and Health*, in the chapter on Practice. This, to my sense, is one of the most important things in all of Mrs. Eddy's writings, and one which is the least understood. It brings out more clearly than anything else the fact that the carnal mind is separate and distinct from mortal man, and that the carnal mind's ideal man is a perfect physicality, free from sickness and sin. In this trial mortal man is represented or depicted in his primitive state as a perfect physical concept. That is, perfect from the standpoint of materiality.

Mortal man is here pictured as residing in mortal body. This mortal body is an object of consciousness. Consciousness constructs its own body. Human consciousness has admitted the beliefs of mortal mind. These beliefs of mortal mind are manifested, or objectified, as body, or the human body. The human body without what Mrs. Eddy terms personal sense is, to human sense, a perfect human body, free from sin and sickness and poverty, and the like. Mortal man, under the supervision of the carnal mind, dwells in mortal body. Along come the arguments of personal sense which the human consciousness admits, and these arguments of personal sense admitted to human consciousness, and, becoming a part of human consciousness, naturally, in turn, become a part of body which is also a part of human consciousness. So one has the ability to choose whether or not he will admit these arguments of personal sense into consciousness, and thereby has the ability to decide whether or not he shall live in a sick human body or a well human body, an inharmonious human body or a harmonious human body. Human consciousness, according to the statements of truth which appear in this "trial," first creates a body in which mortal man resides, or human consciousness resides, and then this human consciousness takes to its concept of body all the arguments of personal sense which produce sickness, poverty, and unhappiness.

In the light of what we have learned about human consciousness — the human mind, the carnal mind, and the divine Mind — I wish you would study carefully this trial in the chapter on Practice. It will unfold to you an entirely new outlook. It is really, to my sense, the summing up, by Mrs. Eddy, of all that she has been trying to convey to us in the previous pages of *Science and Health*. Study this part of *Science and Health* well, dwell upon it, ponder it, digest it, and you will find therein a most precious and wonderful illustration. When we can fully perceive that all that goes to make up material existence exists as one mind outside your and my individual consciousness, and that this mind, through its own thoughts, becomes a part of our individual existence only at our own will or volition, we then begin to see what a wonderful and powerful instrument for good we have with us always. That is, when we realize that everything that exists in our material world, everything that exists in our individual experience, all matter, all material phenomena, is simply the result of the carnal mind held in individual consciousness, and that we have the privilege and power to exclude that carnal mind from our consciousness and in place thereof put the divine Mind, we begin to realize the wonderful opportunity which lies at the door of our thinking for bringing out good and peace and harmony in our everyday experiences. And in this understanding lies the explanation of how Christian Science heals the ills of matter, even though God knows nothing about matter or about the ills of matter.

The Carnal, Human, and Divine Explained

This seems to be a hard thing to understand. I used to think that it was an easy thing to explain understandingly, and that once explained, it would need no further explanation. But I find that it requires constant explanation, and even then I discover that my explanations do not seem to always carry the clear and final word. But it is really simple. Here, we will say by way of explanation, is a human consciousness. Now, without this human consciousness, or outside this human consciousness there is no material world. Matter does not exist independently of your and my thinking. If everyone in the world stopped thinking materially, right then material existence and matter would cease to exist.

Now, your material thinking does not create my material world, and my material thinking does not create your material world. In other words, the sum total of carnal thought does not go to make up a material world. It is individual thought which creates matter, and therefore creation is individual, and not collective. You and I, as I have explained before, are not born into a material world which has been created by the sum total of carnal thinking for ages. You and I create our own worlds by our own thinking, and so far as each individual consciousness is concerned, there is no material world outside individual consciousness.

Those elements of the carnal mind called personal sense are, in turn, reflected as matter in the universe of matter which the individual consciousness is weaving about itself, and therefore each individual consciousness creates its own environment and is responsible for its own world and its own experience. And inasmuch as each individual consciousness is responsible for its own world and its own individual experiences, each is likewise responsible for its own salvation from sin, sickness, inharmony, etc. The inharmony of each individual experience, or existence, exists in the mind of the individual. The carnal in our thinking enables us to see inharmony in others and in the world about us. You and I could not be conscious of sickness or sin or inharmony or floods or cyclones or drought except with the carnal in our thinking. These conditions do not exist in the divine Mind, or God, and therefore to the extent that the divine takes the place of the carnal in our thinking, will these conditions cease to exist in our experience.

Weather Subjective

Mrs. Eddy once said to a class of students in her home (I am not quoting this verbatim) "You have the power and ability to move your arm wherever you wish because your arm is the object of your own thinking or state of consciousness. Therefore you have the same ability to control the clouds, as the clouds are as much an object of individual thought as the arm." So do you not see what a powerful instrument for good lies right here and now in our laps? And in these times of drought, storms, etc., which, in themselves, are nothing more than reflections of the disturbed and barren thought of mankind today, it is incumbent on each and everyone of us to so conduct his thinking that these vehicles of waste and destruction shall not interfere with our individual harmony and prosperity. We cannot work out the salvation of others, but we certainly can and should protect ourselves from the effects of the world's wrong thinking.

Drought and storms and pestilence are not the direct results of thought about droughts and storms and pestilence in the consciousness of mortals, because no mortal wants to become the victim of drought and storm and pestilence. But the barrenness of human consciousness is bound to be expressed in barrenness of earth, because the earth and all therein materially is simply the manifestation of thought. An individual consciousness barren of spiritual things, of peace, love, purity, cannot be conscious of peace and love and purity in its own creation. We cannot be conscious of that which does not exist in thought, because thought is existence. Our visible world is simply our own thoughts objectified. A consciousness which does not contain love could not experience love in its world of environment. A consciousness which knows not peace could not see peace in the world of its own creating. A consciousness devoid of spirituality and purity would be conscious of nothing but grossness and impurity in the world of its own creating.

And so a world consciousness, a national consciousness, which is barren of the spiritual, pure, holy — the things of God — could not expect to experience aught but poverty, unhappiness and misery. A consciousness which would find it possible or which would tolerate or even conceive of the willful destruction of animal life, of wheat, corn, cotton, the fruits of honest labor and toil, for the furtherance of a political whim, should not be surprised at, or complain of a condition of weather which would manifest itself as a devastating drought. Exactly the same thought is responsible for both conditions, although we call one an act of man and the other an act of providence. A drought may eventuate as an act of providence if those who suffer thereby learn their lesson. If they do not learn their lesson through suffering, they will have to suffer still more.

But you and I do not have to suffer because of the shortcomings and misdeeds of others. If we did, where would be our God? And if we did, wherein would lie the fruits of our understanding of Christian Science? If the world suffers because of a drought, the world must look to matter for its remedy. But it does not suffer because of drought. It suffers because of its wrong thinking. If it resorts to matter and material remedies for its answer to the problem of drought, lack, unemployment, etc., it is hewing out empty cisterns made with hands, cisterns which contain no water for the parched earth. But if it turns to God and away from matter and material remedies, then will it be blessed with showers of Spirit and the abundance of God will replenish the whole earth. It is our duty, as Christian Scientists, to prove to the world what an understanding of God can do in this wilderness of blasted human hopes.

Mrs. Eddy often urged upon her household the necessity of overcoming the belief of weather and of handling the arguments of the elements which find expression in storm and tempest, blight and drought. And she never taught them to "work on the weather." She taught them to work for the harmony of divine Mind. Rain and sunshine are alike manifestations of the carnal mind, and as such, they can be regulated by that consciousness which understands how to take away from these carnal beliefs the elements of discord, harm and disruption. To know that God is eternally in His holy temple, and that therefore harmony and abundance reign here and now, is depriving our material picture, the picture the carnal mind has painted for us, of those beliefs of inharmony which would render sun and rain harmful.

There are times according to human beliefs when mankind needs the sun, and there are times when he needs the rain. You and I would not wish our work to deprive anyone of that which he seems to need to complete his sense of joy and fruition; and by knowing that everything is, here and now, eternally in its right place; that God knows naught but harmony; that harmony reigns here and now; and that all man needs is already supplied and in its right place, we can take away from the belief of weather that which mortal mind says would make for inharmony.

The picture which you and I have painted with our carnal thoughts includes the belief of matter, of weather, sunshine and rain. All of these go to make up a materially harmonious whole.

Aside from these, there exists in our picture the belief of inharmony, too much rain, too much sunshine or too little rain. Those conditions are the results of inharmony in our own thinking; and through the understanding of the omnipotence of God and His kingdom, and the presence of right ideas here and now, we are going to be able to so regulate our thinking that the beliefs of inharmony are done away with, and we have a harmonious materiality. By knowing that God reigns; that His kingdom is perfect; that there is nothing in existence but the divine Mind and His ideas governed and controlled by the Mind that created them; that harmony reigns here and now; that there is a supply for every demand and a demand for every supply; that one idea cannot be out of place for one single moment; that the perfect harmony and equipoise of spiritual existence reign here and now; that there is no mortal mind belief, no universal belief, no argument of sign or seasons or superstition, no curse, no penalty of belief which can interfere with or disturb the perfect harmony of existence, we will bring out the expression of harmony in our belief of weather.

Weather might be said to be a primary belief, harmonious and harmless. Then along come the secondary beliefs of mortal mind such as the beliefs of animal magnetism, seasons, fear, hate, anger, and malice, and these beliefs operating in consciousness create what might be termed bad weather or a bad season. It is with weather and climate just as it is with the body. We must bring out in our everyday experience a harmonious body as well as a perfect concept of climate and weather. "Heat and cold," Mrs. Eddy tells us, "are products of mortal mind." (*Science and Health*) By knowing that the only atmosphere there is, is the atmosphere of Truth, and the only climate there is, is the climate of Soul in which is no inharmony, harm or danger, we will handle the beliefs of extremes which mortal mind has attached to the belief of weather or climate.

We must understand that man, in the image and likeness of God, lives, moves and has his being in the atmosphere of Love, of divine Mind, divine intelligence, and that man can be conscious of nothing that does not proceed from that divine Mind. Therefore man cannot be conscious of the belief of bad weather or cold weather or hot weather. These are creations of a mind which does not exist, which God knows nothing about, and concerning which man, in the image and likeness of God, is not cognizant. Always make your mental and oral declarations of Truth in the absolute. There are no relative positions or conditions in Science. Man is either a perfect, spiritual likeness of Spirit, or he is wholly material without a hope in the world. Man is perfect. He is not growing out of a state of imperfection into a state of perfection. He is here and now perfect, and the recognition of this in consciousness is necessary to the proper application of Truth. In working for yourself or for others, do not dwell in the relative. You would not think of God as anything but perfect. And so you must not think of man, yourself, as anything less perfect than God. What you claim about and for God, you may claim about and for yourself.

Demonstration of Abundance

Always know that you have here and now abundance. I wonder if you all appreciate the necessity of declaring the truth about yourself daily in regard to all matters. It is the constant dropping of the water that wears away the stone, and it is, likewise, the constant declaration of Truth about yourself, even in the face of its material opposite, that eventually wins the crown of demonstration. Always declare that you are here and now the full and complete expression of God's abundance. Think, even materially, in large terms. A man certainly cannot demonstrate in terms of hundreds or thousands while thinking in terms of ones and twos. Think in terms of infinity. "Hitch your wagon to a star." Let your human ambitions be fetterless and boundless. That is, let your thinking be in unlimited terms. A man in business could never demonstrate any farther than his thoughts would permit. If a man had a business and his ambition was to bring that business up to a certain limit of production, that limit would be about as far as he would be permitted to go. Even though he never gained the limit of his ambition, it is safe to say that he would not have done as well as he did if his limit had been a small one.

Think in terms of infinity. Know that God's abundance and supply know no bounds or limitation. Always declare in your daily work and thinking for abundance, even in the face of bitter lack. Lack is an argument of mortal mind. Abundance is a reality of God. Always think on the side of God. Discouragement is the clearest evidence of a limited thought. Discouragement is simply mortal mind's way of capitulating to the adversary. It is mortal mind's way of agreeing with lack and limitation. Never submit to it. It will flee from you if you meet it on its own ground and destroy it. It will stay with you and grow and become magnified if you harbor it in thought. You cannot declare for abundance if you admit discouragement into your consciousness. Discouragement and lack come from one and the same source — the carnal mind existing outside human consciousness — and you and I have the privilege of accepting or rejecting them just as we please. If we meet the argument of fear with the idea of courage; the argument of discouragement with the declaration of our independence as children of God; the arguments of lack with the constant declaration of abundance and infinite supply, sooner or later we will bring out in our daily experience exactly what we have been faithfully mentally declaring.

I would love to see my students bring out a better sense of supply. I suppose it is quite natural that I should wish that, but I know positively that none of us is accomplishing along that line what he is capable of accomplishing. We have given in to the argument of limited supply and limited opportunities to a large extent because of the stress of present times, because it is easier to agree with the argument than it is to fight it.

But you and I have got to rise above this and know that we can carry more than our share of the burden which is going to be required of us; that God's abundance is unlimited and that His hand is not withheld. We must watch lest we let in the sense of discouragement, resentment, and disappointment which the present condition of affairs would try to bring to us. With God all things are possible; and certainly you and I are not going to be able to meet our share of the obligation, or rise above the sense of discouragement and disappointment, or enlarge our outlook to the extent of seeing above and beyond these material limitations, unless we enlarge our concepts of God and man in God's image. We must put away all thought of self, of discouragement and limitation, and know that God's child knows no limitations and no boundaries. Think in big terms. Be charitable. Be frugal. Be economical. And above all, know that it is your own constant declaration of abundance and infinite supply that is going to free you from all of the mundane and curtailing arguments of material existence.

We hear much these days about the new order of things, that the day of individualism is past; that we shall hereafter be relieved of the necessity of doing our own thinking; that hereafter all thinking, planning and activity shall be governed by a mental hierarchy which shall do our thinking, planning, acting for us. If there is anything brought out in the Christianity of Jesus Christ more clearly than the necessity for pure individualism, I do not know what it is. Our world, experience, environment, sin, sickness, our very existence, are strictly individual. Existence in all of its phases is individual, and therefore our salvation must be individual. Anything which would teach you and me that the day of rugged individualism is past, is gross heterodoxy.

Inasmuch as we create our own individual worlds by our own individual thinking, it is only in compliance with the law of Principle, the law of God, that our individual world should be governed and regulated by our individual thinking, and so it is. Do you think that existence or salvation could ever become vicarious? That anyone else in all this world could work out our individual problems for us? That anyone else could plan our daily vocations, our daily activities, our methods of work, our plans of living, our individual selections of planting, reaping and harvesting? What does the Bible tell us? "Work out your own salvation with fear and trembling." It does not say that someone else shall do our thinking, planning, planting, and harvesting for us. The very moment you and I permit ourselves to be drawn into the enticing net of letting others do our thinking for us, just then have we delegated to others any hope of success, growth or salvation.

Christianity, or Christian Science, is the very antithesis of a regimented or a bureaucratically controlled world. If you and I are going to insist that we shall go to heaven the way we want to go, rather than by the route of Roman Catholicism, Episcopalianism, Methodism, or whatnot, we are likewise going to be presented with the necessity of declaring our freedom in more material things and insist that we shall work, employ or be employed, plant, sow and reap just as divine Love directs us to, and not be supervised, regulated, regimented, dictated to, curtailed or enjoined by someone else. There is no more necessity in working out our own salvation, free and unhampered by dictation, domination or regimentation, in connection with our religious life than there is in our everyday business affairs. Our material or worldly surroundings are no less under the mercy, supervision and control of our own individual wishes and thinking than are our affairs of religion and salvation. If you and I create our material surroundings by our own individual thinking, how are we to regulate and control those material surroundings by God in consciousness, if we delegate our thinking in regard to those matters to someone else, to someone who knows nothing about God and whose highest concept of authority might consist in "cracking down" on those of his fellow citizens who knew more of God in one minute than he would ever know? My students, do think for yourselves. Do not be led by the whims and wiles of the carnal mind. Square all your thinking with Principle. Measure all things with the tape of Truth, and you will not be led astray.

Daily Prayer for Government

We should all know daily the truth about government. We should work for government. Mrs. Eddy tells that she worked daily for the government, and it is evident that she intended that all of us should do likewise. Our work for government, as in all other things, should be in the absolute. We should know that there is but one government — the government by Mind of all its vast creation of ideas. We should recognize the divine Mind, or divine intelligence, the divine *esse* of all existence, as the only cause and creator, and that the manifestation or outcome of this divine Mind, this one supreme consciousness are ideas. We should know everyday that these ideas are created, controlled, governed, directed, outlined, placed and activated by this one all-knowing, all-seeing, all-wise intelligence. Intelligence, in and of itself, is creator, director, governor and administrator of all law and order. We should know that in the realm of the real (and that is the only realm there is, and that realm is here and now), we live, move, and have our being; that in this realm, everything is idea, and idea is an expression of an all-seeing and all-knowing intelligence; that because of this, all time and place and space are done away with as objects of matter and material phenomena, and in their place there is only idea. We must know that this truth about government is the truth about God and man in God's image and likeness. Man is in his right place here, now and eternally. Man is governed, controlled, directed, supplied and protected by that Mind of which he is the expression. Man can express and be conscious of naught that does not come from his Principle, God. Therefore, man is the expression of God's government, God's law, and God's dominion. The only community there is, is the community of right ideas; the only state there is, is the state of spiritual consciousness; and the only nation there is, is the nation of spiritual ideas created, governed and controlled by the one and only intelligence.

This knowing must not be a mere oral or mental repetition of phrases. This knowing must be based on the understanding that material existence is no existence; that it is a creation of illusion; that it is a state of mesmerism or self-hypnotism; that it is a dream which is the result of a mind which does not exist; and as "the dream and dreamer are one," as Mrs. Eddy tells us in *Science and Health*, and this dream and dreamer are one in a consciousness which does not exist, then there is no state of material consciousness, and the true and spiritual becomes the only real, ever present, tangible state of existence.

In the realm of the material, the government of a nation is divided into the executive, the legislative, and the judicial branches. In Mind, all of these combine in the one all-knowing intelligence, which intelligence finds expression in your and my experience in our right thinking. Thus through our right thinking do we bring out in our own individual lives and experiences the true sense of the executive, legislative, and judicial. Mind creates all. It is the one and only legislator of its own vast array of laws and regulations. Mind executes these laws of its own creating, thus becoming the one and only executive, and by the enforcement of these laws through Principle, right for right, wrong for wrong, Mind thus becomes the only judiciary there is. Thus we have the executive, legislative, and judicial all combined in one intelligence, and this intelligence being the only intelligence there is, can know nothing of any opposite or opposing intelligence or jurisdiction.

The jurisdiction of Mind governs, includes and comprehends all existence, being and reality. Therefore there is no opposing intelligence, disrupting intelligence, conflicting intelligence in government, or in the jurisdiction of Mind. Thus we can say with authority, conviction and finality that there is no belief of dishonesty, greed, graft, trickery, intrigue, either material, personal or mental, that can interfere with, or come within, the jurisdiction of the government of Mind. There is but one Mind, therefore there are not minds many, wills many, purposes many, differences of opinions, misunderstandings or misdirection in government. There is nothing hidden that shall not be revealed in government. Government is here and now revealed to man, and therefore there are no hidden forces, no occult, dishonest, tricky or greedy forces in government which can operate to disrupt, disorganize or destroy.

It is my opinion that the world is not yet even minutely awake to the hidden, corrupt, occult, secret and malicious forces which are constantly directed mentally and materially against modern governments, with the direct purpose to confuse by strife, poverty, wars, hatreds, misunderstandings, and the like. There is no question in my mind but that age-old forces, mental in their nature, are constantly at work to overthrow and confuse modern society to the extent of bewilderment and despair. If this hidden and secret thought can get nations into the mental state of confusion as to the right remedy out of its difficulties; into the mental state of darkness, hopelessness, bewilderment and hatred into which this country of ours has been plunged for some years past, it is beginning to accomplish its purpose. Disasters, calamities and the like, from which there is an open and clear way of escape, is not the ultimate of this mental method of secret attack. Disasters from which there seems to be *no escape*, for which there seems to be *no apparent remedy*, are the tools of this deep and far-reaching occultism.

You and I need not be concerned as to its source, its avenues of attack, the channels or *modus operandi* through which it perpetuates itself. What we are concerned with is that clear understanding of God which sees all of these elements of evil mentally directed as no part of the one intelligence which governs and controls all of God's vast universe of ideas. We must learn to mentally banish all of these lies of mortal mind, malicious mental manipulation, to their realm of unreality. Then we shall not accept or fear them, and we shall, at the same time, individually free ourselves from the belief of power and influence which they claim to exert. Spirituality in thought is the greatest protection that mortal man can ever have. A spiritually-minded man will be able to uncover, discern and detect that which a materially-minded man will mentally accept to his own undoing. A spiritually-minded man can see so far beyond the evidence of the senses into the realm of the mental, which is behind the material, that his protection, guidance and acumen far surpass that of the man who is not spiritually equipped. Thus should the Christian Scientist be the best business-man, lawyer, laborer, salesman there is. Spirituality in thought enables one to see beyond the material into the materially mental and thus discern "the signs of the times" far better and far more deeply than the man on the street.

Don't be afraid to be good. Be afraid *not* to be good. If you are active and clear and honest in your mental and spiritual work, you can run circles around the other fellow in any line of work or endeavor, while he becomes dazed, worried, confused and discomforted, wondering what it is all about. Make your Science an enviable thing to all about you, and not something you would like to hide during the week, and only bring out into the light on Sunday morning. The man who knows that two times two is four has a big advantage over the man who believes that two times two is five, and the former is not afraid of his knowledge, nor does he hesitate to assert and prove it all the time.

Know the truth about your government and know that there are no channels, avenues, minds or conditions through which mortal mind can operate to interfere with the true government of Soul, and the full and complete expression of honesty, ability, and spirituality. Know that no mortal mind, operating or claiming to operate through the avenues or channels of the Roman Catholic Church, or the beliefs of occultism of any name or nature, can interfere with, control, regulate or influence the government of Mind over its ideas. Know that you, as the image and likeness of God, are here and now a clear and sure transparency for Truth, and that true government has now its full and complete expression through you, and that all men are God's children, and that all men are governed, controlled and directed by the one pure, divine and holy intelligence.

Rising above the Belief of Age

And now I want to discuss with you the subject of age — old age. This is something concerning which, I am convinced, Christian Scientists are very derelict. I am extremely, profoundly and shockingly impressed, as I go about the country year after year seeing my Christian Science friends whom I have known for years, with the utter disregard with which this phase of the work is looked upon. Without any reason whatever, without the claim of sickness, or impoverishment, I find my Christian Science friends and acquaintances gradually permitting themselves to come under this claim of age and the passage of time. I do not say this in any sense of criticism. I say it with the intent of warning and advising. There is no reason in the world why a healthy, active Christian Scientist should look any older at sixty than at thirty when you come to figure time in the language of mortal mind.

The shocking thing about the situation, as I observe it, is the utter disregard Christian Scientists have for appearance along this line. There is an old saying and none truer that "a man is no older than he thinks." If a man is no older than he thinks, he certainly should not act and conduct himself in a way which will belie his thinking. I have known many Christian Scientists for over thirty-five years. I have known them well and intimately, and they have demonstrated over the belief of sickness and ill health in a most wonderful manner. They have overcome lack and limitation in many of its phases. Yet I have seen them droop and wither under the claim of age and the passage of time, until today instead of being fresh, upright and vigorous workers in the vineyard of the Lord, they are old, worn out and decrepit. And why? Simply because they have not handled the argument of age and time in their work. I don't know what line of thinking or reasoning they pursue, but I presume that they have allowed the thought to hold them that age and death are two of the things which are beyond our present state of understanding, and they have just let the argument of age, birthdays, and time creep in willingly and without any opposition whatever.

The truest way to test a man's thoughts is by his actions. "Actions" it is said, "speak louder than words," and it is so. We may talk about the nothingness of age, about the absence of time and about the ever-presence of youth, but when a man begins to droop and drag around, get slovenly in his appearance and dress, become sluggardly in walk and actions, that is about the best evidence that his talk is a lot of fair seeming, and that he is thinking just the opposite to what he talks. We reflect physically just what we think, not what we say. It is the duty of every Christian Scientist to handle this argument not only in his daily work, but in his actions, in his activities, mannerisms, dress, appearance, and carriage. One cannot think one way and work out an opposite outward appearance. I know Christian Scientists who, the moment they begin to see the trace of gray hairs in their head begin to bewail the facts and appearance of old age and act accordingly. I have seen perfectly well and healthy Christian Scientists, on the approach of mortal mind's argument of passage of time, allow themselves to become stooped, shrunken in chest, without any physical reasons whatever. I have seen them dress old. I've seen them slouch along, lose interest in that which normally one should be interested in. I've seen them change in a minute, almost, at the birth of a grandchild. I have in mind now (and I shouldn't) a perfectly healthy and well Christian Scientist who is so stooped and bent and bedraggled that you would not recognize him as the man of five years ago. And that is simply because he has allowed the argument of years to bear and bow him down.

Why, my friends, there is no reason for this even from a material point of view. If we are going to talk life eternal and against the argument of old age, we must certainly learn to act young. The example of the young girl, given by Mrs. Eddy in our textbook, who was disappointed in love in her youth and because of a mental condition failed to recognize the passage of time and thus retained her youth, is ample proof of the ability of anyone to maintain at least a semblance of youth in face of the mortal mind argument of the passage of time. We cannot think young and act old or look old. And we cannot look old and act old and at the same time think of ourselves as free from the law of age. We must not only constantly declare against the argument of age, passage of time, heredity, in this regard, but we must take all necessary human steps to support our right thinking and to avoid the appearances of age. It is the duty, I believe, of every Christian Scientist, to look as young, attractive, fresh and buoyant as possible. We should, first of all, watch our carriage.

Now this is somewhat material perhaps, but Mrs. Eddy tells us in *Science and Health*, "We must act as possessing all power from Him in whom we have our being." Now we cannot "act as possessing all power from Him in whom we have our being" if we go about looking old and stooped and decrepit. We cannot expect to act young if we dress old and slovenly. We cannot expect to appear young if we withdraw our interest from those things which pertain to activity, vigor and freshness. So watch your carriage. Do not allow yourself to stoop. In the matter of carriage, it is always well to handle heredity.

There is the belief, perhaps, that at the age of forty or fifty, your father or your mother or your grandparents began to develop certain physical characteristics, such as round shoulders, a slouch in their method of walking, an indifferent and careless method of carriage, all of which you begin to manifest as you approach that same age. Handle the belief of heredity, family traits, characteristics and influences in regard to age. Know what your true parentage is; that your Father and Mother are Spirit; that your heritage is spiritual, not material; and that therefore you are under no argument of animal magnetism expressing itself through the belief of inherited tendencies and influences. Know that as a child of God you are now upright, perfect, erect and stately. And act accordingly. To be plain and more or less material, throw back your shoulders, throw out your chest and pull in your stomach all the time, either when sitting or standing. Now that's plain talk. But never mind how plain it is, try it.

You cannot demonstrate health and act sickly. You cannot demonstrate youth and act old. And besides your carriage, watch your personal appearance. You do not have to dress any older now than you did thirty or twenty or even ten years ago. Keep up with the modes. You can always find something in present modes, even though these modes be very trying at times, which will suit your personal requirements. Now, by this I do not mean that we should be extravagant or that we should devote time and money to beautifying our personalities. That is not the point at all. You may need a dress or a suit of clothes or a hat or a pair of shoes. It does not cost any more to buy something that looks well and young and chic than it does to buy something which some clerk might tell you is best suited to a person of your age. When a clerk springs that one on you, don't get mad at the clerk. Just take that as a gentle hint that you are falling down on the demonstration over age, and that it is time for you to get busy and slick up a bit. Don't slouch in your walk or become sluggish. Be spritely. Act sprightly, vigorous and quick. You will be surprised to find how great a difference your activities and actions make in overcoming this argument of age. You have got to act, Mrs. Eddy tells us, just as you try to think. If you will back up your right thinking by your right acting then your demonstration will have begun. Youth is a seductive thing and keeps one alert in its pursuit.

A businessman, to be successful, should never allow the argument of age to make him slothful, sluggish or careless in appearance, in dress or in posture. There is an argument of physiology as well as Science back of this whole question which will help one in his business, his position, his work. The husband and wife should not allow themselves to take on the arguments of age, decrepitude, carelessness and slovenliness simply because the battle of courtship is won. One should not hold to the position that there is no use running for a train after it is caught. Remember that your personal appearance, your carriage, your looks, your uprightness, will have just as much to do with your victory over age as your mental work. I would say they would share in the result about fifty-fifty.

To sit down and work an hour or so trying to know that one is the son of God, pure, upright, bright, vigorous, etc., and then start out to act and walk like some decrepit inmate of a home for old soldiers, wouldn't accomplish anything. I remember one time I seemed to be sick — good and sick — if you could call sickness good. I was too sick, I thought, to sit up, so I lay down and kept down for a day or so. I was trying to work the thing out in Science, but I didn't seem to be accomplishing much. Finally, I got to thinking about this passage from *Science and Health* just quoted, where Mrs. Eddy tells us to "act as possessing all power" from God, and it came to me that I had only half done my work. I had only half completed my treatment. I felt that my treatment had been a good one, and I couldn't figure out why it hadn't worked. Then I saw that, while my treatment had been good, perhaps, I had not been doing my part in acting in accord with what I had been declaring for myself, so in the face of my misery and discomfort, I decided to get up, and act like a man any way, and see if I could not in that way prove the belief to be a lie. I got up and put on my clothes and acted just as I would have acted without the illness and in a short time relief came. I was certain then that by acting as I should, I had routed rather than entertained the argument which had been holding me. It is the same with the argument of age. One can't feel and be young and at the same time admit the arguments of age.

Coming Under the Belief of Astrology

There is another argument of animal magnetism which one should handle regularly, and which I judge is not given a great deal of attention by Christian Scientists, and that is the argument of astrology — laws of astrology or planetary control. These laws come under or are found included in the practice of horoscope reading. The laws of planetary control or influence are, to material sense, as strong and as binding as are the laws of heredity. As long as man is supposed to live in the flesh, just so long as he is manifesting the beliefs of a material father and mother, and as long as one is laboring under the material argument of material father and mother, just so long will one be under the necessity of handling and meeting the claim of heredity. It is the same with the arguments or beliefs of astrological control.

To illustrate what a fixed and complete science this claims to be, in almost any public library today, you will find books on the subject which were, perhaps, printed before you were born. These books contain charts or tables which will give your exact mental and physical characteristics, tendencies, and so on. That is, astrology is so fixed that one versed therein, if given the day of your birth, can turn to these tables and charts and tell you unerringly what your mental and physical tendencies are, what particular physical ailments you are subject to, what physical characteristics hold you, what mental idiosyncrasies may be binding you, etc.

This science holds that everyone born into the world is born under the influence of certain planets or planetary conditions; that there is an electromagnetic influence existing constantly governed by the location and position of the various planets, and that this influence changes daily with the revolutions of the earth and the movement of the various stellar systems, planets, etc.; that this electromagnetic influence governs and controls everything; and that a person born today, for instance, is governed throughout his entire life by the planetary influences as they exist on the day of his birth. Certain zodiacal signs and conditions are believed to control and influence, through the existence of this electromagnetic current, everyone who is born under these signs and conditions, and this law is so fixed and active that one familiar with it can foretell unerringly the exact mental and physical conditions of one so born. And everyone of us is claimed to be born under the control or influence of some planet or combination of planets. So do you not see the constant necessity of handling and meeting this claim of animal magnetism calling itself astrology, planetary control, horoscopic influence?

One should know constantly that matter has no mind, hence no intelligence to control man; that man was never born; that man is the spontaneous expression of Spirit and is under the constant influence and control of his spiritual parentage; that there is no intelligent matter which can create, transmit or receive; that there is no influence or condition which can create magnetism or electricity which can govern and control man; that man is a free, independent, spontaneous expression of the one and only intelligence which knows and governs its own vast creation of ideas in perfect harmony; that there is no combination of material influences or conditions, either of a positive or a negative nature, which can operate to produce an electromagnetic current to govern man; that man is not independent of God; that man is God expressed and therefore is not subject to any of the beliefs of matter or intelligent matter. Matter cannot think or act or create. Error has no origin, no place of origin, no medium or type of expression.

Electricity

You must understand the importance of handling this claim of electricity constantly. If this is done, I am sure you will find many things will be eliminated as problems which have heretofore appeared adamant.

In the first place, we should recognize the fact that all material life is claimed to be the product of electricity. Years and years ago, Mrs. Eddy saw and recognized this, and she was ridiculed and criticized by the world of natural science and medicine for it. Today, the natural scientist has resolved all matter into positive and negative electrical forces and asserts electricity to be the ultimate or remote cause of matter. In *Science and Health* Mrs. Eddy says: "Knowing the claim of animal magnetism, that all evil combines in the belief of life, substance, and intelligence in matter, electricity, animal nature, and organic life, who will deny that these are the errors which Truth must and will annihilate?"

Here, Mrs. Eddy uses "electricity," matter and "organic life" synonymously. Thus we find that organic life, or the belief of life, truth, intelligence and substance as existing in matter, is synonymous with electricity. And what does she say about electricity? That is, what is it? In *Science and Health* she tells us that "Electricity is not a vital fluid, but the least material form of illusive consciousness — the material mindlessness which forms no link between matter and Mind, and which destroys itself." And, "Electricity is the sharp surplus of materiality which counterfeits the true essence of spirituality or Truth, the great difference being that electricity is not intelligent, while spiritual truth is Mind." Here she refers to electricity as "material mindlessness," taking away from electricity even the claim of a mortal mind which does not exist.

I think one of the best things Mrs. Eddy ever penned in regard to this subject of electricity is to be found in the Third Edition of *Science and Health*, where she says: "One of the material forces counterfeiting Truth is electricity. Is it not significant that despite an extensive and practical working knowledge of electricity, physical science remains ignorant of what that force actually is? Christian Science discloses that since electricity is material, its essence must be mortal mind, because matter is the expression of mortal mind, and Christian Science further declares that whatever the employment of electricity has done to advance the human race, is but the counterfeit of the genuine unfoldment of spiritual truth in consciousness. Thus considered, all material progress, in reversal, reveals spiritual unfoldment. So in human consciousness, electricity, radioactivity, and the more recent theories and developments and prospects of inter-atomic force, are typical of the evolution of human thought out of itself. The more matter is displaced in favor of its essence, mortal mind, the thinner mortal mind's mask becomes, for remember — mortal mind cannot express itself save as matter.

"Electricity is not a vital fluid, but an element of mind, the less material thought that forms the link between what is termed matter and mortal mind; but recollect that both are strata of belief, the one called mind and the other called matter; the grosser substratum, named matter, is the poorest counterfeit of Mind; the more ethereal substratum of mortal belief, named mind, is the nearer counterfeit of immortal Mind or Truth or Love; but both are false presentations, for immortal Mind and mortal belief never touch.

"The electricity of mortal mind, its gases and forces are the counterfeits of the unerring and eternal Mind's omnipotence as Truth, its attraction as Love, and its adhesion and cohesion as Life, producing the eternal Mind, termed Holy Ghost, the great difference being that one is divine and Holy, and the other human and unholy."

Electricity, we thus find to be a manifestation of mortal mind. And how is mortal mind manifested to you and me? Why, as matter. Does mortal mind operate to create matter outside your and my individual consciousness? We have learned that it does not. Whence then does matter come from? It comes from the carnal or mortal mind which you and I admit into our individual consciousness and which, in turn, is projected or objectified as matter. Electricity being then a material manifestation of the carnal mind and mortal thought, whence comes electricity? Why, from individual thought. And as we begin to endow thought with spiritual intuitions and concepts, do you not see we can begin to control and regulate our concepts of electricity to the extent of taking away from it the belief of harm and injury, and making it a useful and helpful part of our experience?

We have seen that, through the right understanding of Truth, we should be able to regulate and control the weather, the clouds, the climate, etc. In like manner, we should be able to control and regulate the belief of electricity, as electricity is just as certainly a mani-festation of individual, material thinking as any other form of materiality. Recognizing that electricity, like any other form of matter, is the product of individual thought, we can begin to overcome the arguments of electricity by watching thought. Electricity is brought into action materially by friction. Therefore, that which tends to mental friction, irritation, etc., might be considered as the foundation of electrical phenomena. We should handle static or electromagnetism.

The material theory is that electricity exists in what might be termed solution throughout space without material manifestation, but that through certain material conditions or activities (friction) this element is brought into action. This inactive electricity is called static. This might be termed unconscious mind or thought. Electric or static magnetism expresses itself through the medium of friction, and is influenced in material theories by the state of atmosphere or climatic conditions. You will find that by handling the claim of electricity, static or electro-magnetism, in cases of skin disease, eczema, deafness, irritation, etc., you will meet with much more success than ordinarily.

In *Science and Health* Mrs. Eddy quotes Mesmer as follows: "There exists a mutual influence between the celestial bodies, the earth, and animated things. Animal bodies are susceptible to the influence of this agent, disseminating itself through the substance of the nerves." Now if this is so in a material sense, you and I are in a position to determine just where this power or influence arises because we know that there is nothing material but what comes from individual thought. Therefore, our remedy is knowing the truth and denying the error in our own consciousness, thereby handling the claim where it originates — in individual thought. We must deny that the earth's magnetic currents can control or govern man, or regulate his life and prospects. Deny animal attraction and material substance. The argument of sex and all pertaining thereto has its foundation in the belief of electricity, and friction.

"Adhesion, cohesion and attraction," Mrs. Eddy tells us in *Science and Health*, "are properties of Mind." I have seen a quotation purporting to come from the pen of our Leader, as follows: "Electricity is the thought essence which forms the link between matter and mortal mind. God, the divine Mind, self-existent, self-perpetuating and self-energizing, is the great universal reservoir or dynamo, and the thoughts which flow from such fountains constituting a complete expression of the infinite Mind, Spirit, are thus shown to be inseparably linked with the Principle of Life, and action to be the manifestation of force or power."

In the tenth chapter of Luke we read: "And the seventy returned unto him with joy, saying Lord, even the devils are subject unto us through thy name. And he said unto them, I beheld Satan as lightening fall from heaven. Behold, I give unto you power to tread on serpents and scorpions, and over all the power of the enemy: and nothing shall by any means hurt you."

And in *Science and Health* we read: "A knowledge of error and of its operations must precede that understanding of Truth which destroys error, until the entire mortal, material error finally disappears, and the eternal verity, man created by and of Spirit, is understood and recognized as the true likeness of his Maker."

And are we not now beginning to gain some understanding of that which has heretofore appeared to mankind as a mystery, thereby gaining a victory over what has appeared to be the inevitable and unavoidable? It is mysticism which has given mesmerism and hypnotism and spiritualism the power over mortals which they seem to have had. And now the guise is being stripped from the face of all these seeming unexplainable things by the truth of spiritual perception and understanding. False systems resort to mysticism in their activities in order to hold the awed respect of otherwise sane and normal men and women, and it is the universal sense of awe and fear of what is not understood, which constitutes and maintains the supposed power possessed by them with which to work mischief. When the mysticism is gone, their power is gone, and your work is done.

Jesus said: "I beheld Satan as lightning." He could have said, and undoubtedly meant: "I beheld Satan as electricity," for that was about the only form of electricity the world was familiar with in those days. From what Mrs. Eddy has written in *Science and Health* above quoted, or referred to, it is evident that our Leader knew the true import of this saying of Jesus; and she evidently recognized that to successfully meet its claims to power, it is of vital importance to comprehend the *modus operandi* and the natural laws of this force. Physicians and physical scientists have quite generally adopted the theory which explains away matter, declaring it to be merely a condition of electric magnetism. Now we know in truth that the creations of God are positive. The only positive, eternal and vital force in the realm of the real is God and His creation, man and the universe. Therefore, man is the positive of creation.

Mortal mind in its material theories, in its attempted counterfeit of the spiritual or real, creates matter, including man, as the negative pole of electrical force. The opposite of the positive of Spirit, must be the negative of matter. All matter, then, under the law of reversal becomes negative electricity. This condition, being the outcome of a mind which does not exist, becomes mindless. Therefore if we are to take away from matter or electricity the destructive and creative force with which error would endow it, we must recognize it as mindless, Godless, and Christless as to quality or quantity. Electricity cannot show itself without magnetism. Electricity is the reaction or reflection on a lower plane of the agency called magnetism. Electricity is magnetism and magnetism is the life of matter. Magnetism is the mindless counterfeit of Life, God. In mindless subservience to intelligence, this natural law of magnetism or electricity renders possible our modern telephone, electric light, radio, and so on. Under proper control this tremendous power available to man through this agency becomes as "harmless as a dove."

Each one of us should know daily that man is the positive of Spirit; that man cannot be negatively electrified; that man is the positive expression of the one and only force or power; that the great creative and promulgating dynamo of infinite Spirit is here and now expressed through man; and that there are no negative forces operative to deny and nullify the positive activities and manifestations of Truth. Handle the argument of electricity, negative electrification, etc. in the case of friction in your home, difficulties in your church, in your business relations, etc. Friction is the foundation for electricity which disrupts the calm spiritual existence unless met and handled. Know that "the calm, strong currents of true spirituality," as Mrs. Eddy has put it in *Science and Health*, are the only true and life-giving currents, and that these currents of life and love cannot be interfered with, disrupted or nullified by the arguments of electricity. Matter is no obstacle to Truth. Truth is infinite, everywhere present and is ever active. Watch your innermost thoughts lest they be such as engender friction, etc. Friction is mental, and friction causes the phenomena of electricity.

The time for closing has come. I hope I have not wearied you with too much talking. Christian Science is vast. It is exhaustless. But, while the understanding of being involves eternal spiritual unfoldment in individual consciousness, let us not be confused nor discouraged by its vastness and its infinity. Let us rather rejoice in the fact that at last we have found the way; that we have entered the straight and narrow path, and let us resolve to hold to that path and not be led into the byways of materiality by the lures and wiles of a better road, an easier way. Nothing is gained in the world without struggle, sacrifice and faithfulness; and, likewise, nothing is accomplished in the struggle for spiritual bliss without work and devotion and consecration to that which we know to be the true way in Christian Science.

During the past few years I have been presented with the question as to what attitude we as Christian Scientists should take in regard to smoking, drinking light wines, beers, etc. Among Christian Scientists I have been told that even Christian Scientists indulge in what they call "harmless pastimes" on the ground that one must avoid being narrow and bigoted; that one should be broad, and that a cigarette now and then, or glass of wine or beer now and then, will not only not harm one, but will make one a good fellow and will attract others to Christian Science who might not otherwise be interested. Well, when they come to me with that kind of stuff, they have come to the wrong man if it is comfort and sympathy with their views that they want.

I will say briefly that if this Christian Science movement is ever lost to the world, it will be lost because of just that kind of people who have gotten into our movement. When they speak to me about an innocent cigarette, a little sip of light wine and beer, they are talking to the wrong man because I have gone down the line with all three in my time and there is not a man, woman or child on the face of the earth who can tell me anything about cigarettes, light wines, beers or any other kind of intoxicating drink. I know them all, and thank God, through Christian Science, they hold no lures or snares for me; and the man who deceives himself with the alibi that they are innocent and harmless, is only fooling himself, and if he happens to be connected in any way with Christian Science, is doing more than anything else to empty our churches and drive people away from this saving Christ.

Of late I have heard many complaints throughout the United States of a falling off in church attendance. I see but one reason for this, and that is the Christian Scientist who has not enough regard for his Church, to say nothing of his own demonstration, to have overcome and put out of his life the use of these useless and harmful stimulants. Doctors and physical scientists now are telling us that a confirmed cigarette smoker is morally dull and is almost invariably bound to be dishonest. You can always test or judge anything by its ultimate. I have seen men just as intoxicated on light wines and beers as on whiskey. The ultimate of all of them is the same. And there is your answer.

MAN – GOD SUSTAINED

Association Address of 1944

The little overcomings in our daily lives are the things which bear fruit and enable us to meet the greater problems when they arise. Always remember that God takes care of the goal; our work is to take care of the pathway leading thereto. The pathway is the preparation we make in our daily consecrated devotion to Truth. Truth is its own impulsion and leads mortals to heights which the human mind cannot encompass.

The Material Universe and the Human Consciousness

Man is an ideal. He is not only idea, but he is an ideal. That ideal is maintained in and by Mind. This is a most important feature to be considered in connection with your work in Christian Science. It is a concept which, if understood clearly in its spiritual import and applied to yourself or your patient, will entirely remove from your consciousness any sense of self-sufficiency, self-support, or self-importance. It will remove any sense of self-responsibility, authority and independence, and will enable you, without reservation, to shift the government to His shoulders, which, in itself, is one of the greatest sources of healing, happiness and contentment.

The whole fabric of mortal existence, as seen from the standpoint of human thinking, consists of the belief that man is separate and apart from God, that he is an independent worker, that he is forever on his own, and that his whole existence must be governed and regulated by a human mind which belongs to him and which is subject to all sorts of limitation, incapacity, and influence over which he, himself, has no control.

This mortal mind, or human consciousness, with which each

individual is possessed and which is the so-called governing influence of his existence, is the avenue through which all human limitations come to mankind. It is supposed to be governed by the laws of heredity, the influence of education, the impressions of material environment, hypnotic suggestion, clairvoyance, etc. Nothing in the whole gamut of mortal existence but comes to us through the human consciousness.

If you, sometime, will take your concordances and look up all that Mrs. Eddy has given us on the "human consciousness" or, to use her other expression, the "human mind," you will be surprised to see to your own satisfaction that everything that is to be accomplished through Christian Science for the salvation of mortals has to do exclusively and entirely with the regeneration of the human consciousness, or human mind. Of course, in the absolute, God knows nothing about the human consciousness or the human mind. For that very reason you and I have got to know about it, what it claims to do for and with mortals, and how to accomplish our freedom from those influences of evil which operate through the human consciousness. In fact, the very basis of healing in Christian Science has to do exclusively with the human consciousness. Healing has nothing to do with sickness, with matter, with the human body, with material symptoms, exposure, contagion or germs. Healing in Christian Science has exclusively to do with the so-called human consciousness, and to ignore that human consciousness in your contemplation and explanation of Christian Science in its application would be like ignoring the science of numbers in the explanation of mathematics. It is only through the human consciousness that the Christ finds expression.

Mrs. Eddy tells us that the human body exists only in the human consciousness and as a manifestation of the human consciousness. If that is so, then a regeneration of the human consciousness is all that is necessary to heal the body. If the human body is the objectified manifestation of the individual human consciousness, then all of the ills of the human body must be the manifestations of that same individual human consciousness. When the individual human consciousness is healed of its belief of sickness, then the human body, which is the objectified manifestation of that human consciousness, is relieved of the belief of sickness and thus we have what Mrs. Eddy terms "a better belief."

In the work of healing, the elimination of a material, erroneous condition is not the objective. Scientifically speaking, there is no material condition to be met, Mrs. Eddy tells us; but that fact cannot be bought out except through a regeneration of the human consciousness. God knows no error. All error exists in the human consciousness, and when the human consciousness through the operation of Truth, becomes divine, the errors of the carnal mind are thus eliminated through the influx of the divine into consciousness. If you realize that material existence, with all of its ills, are the objectified manifestations of the carnal mind operating through the human consciousness, you will then see that the human consciousness, purified and spiritualized by the influx of the divine Mind, will sooner or later become manifested in a world of harmony and peace. As we all know, salvation must be made in progressive footsteps leading out of materiality and up to the throne of God. The throne of God is the divine enthroned in consciousness.

You will recall that Mrs. Eddy says in *Unity of Good*, "The more I understand true humanhood, the more I see it to be sinless, — as ignorant of sin as is the perfect Maker." Now this true state of humanhood to which Mrs. Eddy thus refers, is a state of consciousness which has been the possession of every one of us at one time. Therefore, at some time the objectified manifestations of that state of consciousness in each and every one of us must have been harmonious and without error of any nature except the one error of limitation which made the human body an entity in the existence of each one of us.

This pure state of humanhood to which Mrs. Eddy refers as "sinless," is that state of consciousness which each one of us must strive to attain, or return to, through the ministrations of Christian Science. The journey from our present position of erroneous matter, or inharmonious matter, to the position of true humanhood or harmonious matter, is the journey you and I are now taking. The state of "true humanhood" to which Mrs. Eddy refers in *Unity of Good* could not have been wholly bodiless, from a material point of view, in view of the fact that it included that one error of limitation to which she refers in her definition of Euphrates in *Science and Health*. In this definition, as you know, she uses these statements, "The atmosphere of human belief before it accepts sin, sickness or death; a state of mortal thought, the only error of which is limitation; finity; the opposite of infinity." Now this statement is not made in connection with what she says in *Unity of Good* as to true humanhood; but taken together, they evidently refer to the identical state of consciousness; and because of the fact that this state of consciousness includes the one error of "limitation" or "finity," we are bound to the conclusion that this state of true humanhood must include the belief of a human body without any besetting sin aside from that of limitation. This state of pure humanhood is the state of consciousness to which you and I must return, or which you and I must achieve, before we can accomplish what is commonly known as the ascension.

That state of true humanhood must be a state of bodily existence without sin, sickness, poverty and inharmony of any nature. The journey from our present state to that state of humanhood must be the order of salvation, if Christian Science is scientifically explainable. There must be a state of material perfection to which we must attain before our final demonstration can be made, and this state of material perfection is explained and made possible only through the understanding that all the secondary beliefs of human existence, all sin, sickness, poverty, and discord, have come to us in proportion as we have sullied our true state of humanhood by the admission of the carnal into consciousness.

Thus do we include in our own consciousness that which we see, feel, taste, smell and hear, all of which constitutes that which we shall someday overcome. So you must realize that the substance, the inharmony, the error which we conceive of as belonging to our brother man exists in our own consciousness, and must be overcome in our own consciousness. Harmony in what we call our outside world unfolds itself to you and me only as we spiritualize individual consciousness.

Man — God Sustained

With the understanding that the material universe is a reversal and counterfeit of the real and spiritual, it will be recognized that just as mortal man includes his universe, so man in the image and likeness of God includes his universe of spiritual ideas. Man, God's man, is not an isolated, localized, material manifestation thrust out into a material world with a mind of his own with which he must govern himself. The underlying fallacy of material existence is the argument that man has a destiny to work out for himself, and that he has to work out this destiny with a mind of his own. This mind is subject to all sorts of discords and disorders, and is subject to all the claims and activities of error; and mortal man is endowed with an individual responsibility which eliminates the assistance of any higher power from the general scheme of salvation. The helplessness of mortal man lies in the fact that his salvation rests within himself, and there is nothing within mortal man of a higher nature than mortality itself. Mrs. Eddy speaks of this when she says, "The fountain can rise no higher than its source." Mortal man has nothing within himself by which he can rise any higher than his own mortal consciousness will permit. Hence the necessity of God and His Christ in the process of salvation.

The man of God's creating is an ideal, and this ideal is maintained by the Mind creating it and not by man himself. Therefore, man, as a child of God, has no responsibility, authority or independence of his own. Man has nothing to do about his existence. All creation exists and is maintained in Mind. The truth about God's man is the truth about you and me. God maintains His own ideal in divine consciousness. Entirely separate and distinct from our present state of seeming mortal existence, you and I exist in the divine consciousness, free, holy and spiritual now. We have always existed in the divine consciousness, and always will.

In *The People's Idea of God* Mrs. Eddy says, "Even the pangs of death disappear, accordingly as the understanding that we are spiritual beings here reappears and we learn our capabilities for good, which insures man's continuance and is the true glory of immortality." Speaking spiritually, that divine ideal which is man needs no salvation. Man in God's image and likeness was never thrust out of Spirit or born into matter. Mortal man is not God's man gone wrong. He is mortal mind's own mistaken concept of man. To realize for yourself that you are now held in the divine consciousness as a free, complete and spiritual ideal, and that nothing that you do or say can change that eternal fact, is endowing yourself with that spiritual consciousness which rules out all error. You have nothing to do with the perpetuation of God's ideal. God maintains His own image and likeness. God is the only author. In *Science and Health* Mrs. Eddy says that "Mind forms its own likeness." As there is but one Mind and as Mind knows no opposite or no adulteration, there is no other influence to interfere with the likeness of Mind. So you and I do not have to be concerned about healing God's man. God's man needs no healing. What you and I are concerned with, is getting out of individual consciousness those impressions which hide from us the true ideal. The ideal exists the same yesterday, today and forever, in its eternal and infinite expression without aid or hindrance from you or me. Nothing can ever interfere with your and my perfect state of existence as an ideal in Mind. To realize that we are God's ideal and that God forever maintains that ideal in infinite perfection, is to relieve ourselves of any sense of individual responsibility, care or authority.

We hide from ourselves the concept of our true ideal by conceiving ourselves to be personal or individual originators, actors, thinkers, authors or creators. If we can get the human self out of the way and let God's ideal be manifest in consciousness, then God governs our lives and we do not have to strive. God outlines, inspires and motivates our every action, and so we are free from limitations, mistakes, misguiding and conniving. Wouldn't existence be wonderful if you and I did not have one single responsibility; if we didn't have to make a living; if we didn't have to plan and scrimp and connive; if we didn't have to outline? Why do we have to do all of these things? Simply because we have shut out the true ideal by thinking that we are independent of God and His government. If we can get to the point where we can see ourselves as God sees us, then we can shift the government to His shoulders, and we will cease, then, to make mistakes, to be in a hurry, to be too late or too early, too slow or too fast, to be weary or in want. And all of this can be realized humanly. The beauty of Christian Science is that we do not have to reach the ultimate to enjoy the realities of existence on our pathway upward.

God maintains man, and therefore man is not self-sustained or self-supported. He is not an isolated, circumscribed personality, thrust out on an uncharted sea of error without a guide or comforter. Through the clear realization that man is God's ideal, maintained and existing right here and now in Mind, and not subject to any of the phases of mortality, we can appreciate and appropriate to ourselves the benefits and blessings of the eternal fact that man is God's responsibility. Now, that is not merely a convenient statement. It is a fact which, when realized and appropriated in individual consciousness, will bring more freedom, peace, and calm assurance than anything I know.

Body

Sometime ago I read a long and very much involved metaphysical dissertation on "body," including organs, which article is purported to have been given in an association address. I am not advised as to the author of this article, so I cannot be charged with either professional jealousy or criticism. It went so thoroughly into organs and the metaphysical interpretation thereof that I do not see how anyone listening to the paper could have avoided the mental impression of the reality of a material stomach, or heart, or liver.

All instruction in Christian Science should lead us away from any sense of material organs. If man is spiritual, he is sustained by God, and all of his faculties exist in Mind, and are sustained in Mind, and are not material, functional, or organic. To even attempt to give a spiritual interpretation of heart would be to recognize that there is a spiritual idea of heart back of what mortal mind calls heart. Now, remember this: everything which mortal mind claims to have accomplished through process and organization can be included metaphysically in the one word — *reflection.* That is all that you or I or anyone else has to know about functions or faculties — *reflection.* Nothing is manifested or accomplished through or by man that is not accomplished through reflection, and inasmuch as God maintains His own reflection, the government remains eternally on His shoulders, and there is no responsibility of existence resting on man.

The article I refer to spent a lot of time explaining the spiritual significance of stomach. Well, in the first place, there is no spiritual significance to stomach or any other organ. Reflection is maintained by and in Mind. It is never maintained by man. Reflection includes everything that mortal mind has to accomplish through material process, action, elimination and assimilation. Mortal mind says that digestion involves not only organs, but secretions, acids, fluids, glands, timing, material activity, and so on — operations too numerous to mention. Now to go into all of that from a metaphysical standpoint, and try to metaphysically hookup all of these mortal mind phases with divine activity, would not only be a waste of time, but would evidence a most appalling lack of understanding as to God and His creation.

As to the question of digestion, spiritually speaking, that term is fully and finally taken care of in divine Science in the one word reflection, which leaves it all in Mind and relieves man of any sense of organ or process, spiritual or otherwise. Completion, fulfillment, satisfaction is expressed in man through reflection. That is all the digestion there is, and as man has no responsibility, authority or independence of his own, digestion or reflection does not depend on man, but rests entirely in Mind. We are inclined to overlook the fact, sometimes, that in Mind, in reality, everything is complete, finished and final, and that there is no process, operation, development or change. The calm, strong currents of true spirituality which fill immensity, and which, flowing from God to man, constitute the only reality of existence, are included in reflection and can be considered in the sense of circulation.

Circulation thus resolves itself into reflection, rather than into process. Therefore, there is no such thing as organic propulsion. There is also no such thing as confinement, for Spirit, filling immensity and constituting all substance, removes any sense of localization, limitation, or objectification. If, therefore, there is no organic propulsion and no confinement, there can be no pressure. The human sense of pressure depends on force on one hand and confinement, or opposition to force, on the other. If there is no pressure, (organic propulsion) and no resistance (confinement) then there is no rupture or interference. This realization will handle any argument of high blood pressure, varicose veins, rupture or hernia. You don't have to go into the muck and mire of organs or spiritual organs to realize that all of this lies in reflection, and that reflection is maintained by God and not by man.

"The breath of the Almighty giveth man life," the Bible states. The breath of the Almighty must be divine inspiration which is provided by God. Inspiration, then, constitutes respiration. Respiration is a manifestation of Mind, and Mind is its own atmosphere, weather, temperature, climate and air. Man includes his universe through reflection. Therefore man includes everything that God is conscious of. Consequently man is not hypersensitive to weather, climate, temperature, atmosphere and air because he includes them.

He is not a servant or a slave to anything because he includes all, and he is therefore subject to nothing from without. In fact, there is no such thing as the term without, or outside of, in Science. God and man fill immensity, and there is nothing but Mind and Mind's idea in infinity. There is nothing without or outside God and man. This realization that man includes all that God creates, including Mind's own atmosphere, weather, climate, temperature and air, will handle the argument of hayfever, colds, flu and asthma.

You don't have to delve into organs or the spiritual idea of organs to become clear as to God and man. Every faculty or function of man is a divine idea which God maintains, supports and perpetuates, and therefore man has no faculty or function of his own. He reflects God, and God maintains that reflection. To realize that God is the substance of man, the creator of man, and the perpetuator of man, and therefore maintains man, is a metaphysical realization that will be of much help to you in your work. The divine consciousness which inspires, animates and controls man, also constitutes the substance of man. That is all you have to know to realize the true sense of body. Body is divine consciousness. Man is really the body of God. Don't bother yourself with organs or spiritual organs. Divine consciousness is cause. Divine consciousness is substance. Therefore God is cause as well as substance — the substance of man. From this you can soar into the infinite realm of Mind without the hindering influences of organs, material body, or spiritualized matter.

Some time ago I received the following question from one of the pupils, the answer to which comes in the subject of body more particularly than under any other topic. The question is as follows: "I need to have a clear understanding of how to meet this fashionable belief 'allergies' — which I assume includes hayfever, since that seems to be a response to a weed. Intellectually, I can see how ridiculous it is for man who is 'lord of the belief in earth and in heaven,' to respond and be made miserable by everything from various foods to weeds to damp weather, but I cannot seem to realize the bodily freedom that I am sure is man's by right."

Now, the answer to this question comes in one's understanding of true body. Just as mortal man's world and all that goes to make up that world is the objectified manifestation of individual human consciousness, so the world of the man of God's creating consists of divine ideas which man reflects, and thus does man include his universe. The universe which man includes and over which he is master through reflection, is the body of Christ, and is something which is governed entirely by God. The objects of sense lose all power to harm when we realize that body is universe, and the universe consists of divine ideas which God not only creates, but governs.

The understanding of these truths is the Christ operating in consciousness, and this understanding is in itself the liberator. No human sense of directing a treatment, or of giving a treatment, is requisite to the realization of freedom from error. Understanding, itself, is freedom. Understanding in human consciousness of the truths of being is the Christ, and to be so blind to the teachings of Mrs. Eddy as to fail to recognize the claim of a human consciousness is to miss the very heart and soul of Christian Science. Mrs. Eddy tells us that it is necessary to understand error and its claims before we can heal them. We cannot hide ourselves from these claims of error by a declaration of the absolute without their correlative. Through recognizing that matter and its claims are but the objectified manifestation of the carnal operating through the human consciousness, it becomes perfectly evident that the purification of the human consciousness through the influx of the Christ is our only healer.

Body includes universe, and man includes universe. Therein lies our freedom — in the fact that understanding and understanding alone is the liberator. Try to embody divine perception. Always remember this, that divine consciousness is the only cause there is, and that divine consciousness is the only substance there is. Therefore, consciousness is not only cause; but it is at the same time substance; and cause and substance both being divine and perfect, there are no opposites. The divine consciousness which inspires and animates man constitutes the substance of man. A clear realization of this will heal you of anything, as consciousness thus resolves itself into body. Harmony unfolds itself, but it cannot unfold itself to you and me if we are individually mentally inharmonious. Our own individual sense of inharmony is that which obscures from our vision the divine harmony. Our own clarification of thought removes the mist which hides from us the divine harmony. The divine harmony is always unfolding and unfolded. Unfolding is not a process; it is an accomplished fact in Mind. Mrs. Eddy also says, "Mind forms its own likeness," which means that Mind not only forms its own likeness, but maintains that likeness throughout eternity. Thus is man relieved of any sense of responsibility, authority or independence of his own. Leave it to God, and He will bring it about.

Letting Spirit Bear Witness

One pupil writes, "In Science and Health, Mrs. Eddy has written, 'If Spirit, or the power of divine Love bear witness to the truth, this is the ultimatum, the scientific way, and the healing is instantaneous.' Please enlarge on this, and explain this to us so that our healing work will be more instantaneous."

Healing, or treatment, lies in the consciousness of the healer. All the errors of which the healer is conscious lie in his own consciousness. The material world of the healer is the objectified manifestation of the material in his own consciousness. As the materiality of the healer is neutralized and changed by the admission of the divine into consciousness, the material world of the healer becomes less material until he sees with scientific and spiritual certainty the spiritual facts of being. This spiritual clarification of thought on the part of the practitioner constitutes what Mrs. Eddy terms above as letting "Spirit or the power of divine Love bear witness to the truth." If the practitioner is thinking and living constantly in this higher realm of spiritual consciousness then there is no cloud of material thinking to be removed by the practitioner before he can gain that clear consciousness which heals.

If the consciousness of the practitioner is filled with the cares of this world, material cares, material concerns, planning, outlining, fearing and fussing, then "the Spirit or power of divine Love," is not bearing witness and the healing is slow and prolonged — the length of time depends on the length of time it takes for the practitioner to rid himself of those thoughts and concerns which tend to hinder the clear perception of Truth. If the practitioner is living in the constant consciousness of Truth, letting "Spirit or the divine power" bear constant witness, then when a patient comes to him with a claim of mortal mind to be healed, the practitioner's consciousness is so in line with the infinite that the claim which the patient has brought, finds no admission to the practitioner's consciousness because of his clear spiritual perception, and therefore there is nothing to be healed, as far as the practitioner is concerned, and the claim is met. It is only to the extent that the error which is brought by the patient finds admission to the consciousness of the practitioner that the healing is prolonged. Thus both the claim which the patient brings to be healed and the healing, lies wholly with the practitioner; and the practitioner who is constantly dwelling in the secret place of the most high — that is, the practitioner who is constantly letting "Spirit or the power of divine Love bear witness," — is the practitioner who will have the instantaneous healing.

Thoughts of materiality do not bear witness to "Spirit or the power of divine Love." The only place the claim as patient exists, is in that human consciousness calling itself practitioner or healer. The belief of patient is just as much a claim of mortal mind as is sickness, so the consciousness which calls itself healer or practitioner must become free of the belief of patient in order to heal. Consciousness becomes free of the belief of patient by constantly dwelling in the realization of God and God's man. That is, being God's man instead of just thinking about God and man. In the realm of Truth, it is obvious there could be no claim of patient and no claim of sick patient. Naught but the absolute must command the thought and perception of the healer. In the absolute there is no healer, but to ignore the human concept and its need for healing, even though Truth is absolute, would deprive suffering humanity of that for which Jesus came to us, and to which the Bible and *Science and Health* are dedicated.

Materially speaking, you are your own consciousness. All there is to you is your consciousness of yourself, or more particularly speaking, your own consciousness. Your self is your consciousness. Speaking in the spiritual absolute, man — and that is you in reality — is the consciousness of God expressed. The consciousness of God expressed is not voluntary on the part of God's man. Man is an involuntary expression of the divine consciousness. Hence God expresses Himself as man, and man has no will or volition of his own, and man cannot help being as perfect as his Maker. Man has no part to play in expression. Expression is wholly the manifestation of God's will. Therefore to gain a clear sense of our true selfhood is to sweep away the clouds and cobwebs of a selfhood apart from God, and let "Spirit or the power of divine Love bear witness."

HEALING IS IN INDIVIDUAL CONSCIOUSNESS

Association Address of 1941

The Evolution of Mankind

Throughout history men have gotten so far away from God and the spiritual teachings of the Bible that there was little in experience that bore the stamp of purity and holiness; and when there was left little in human consciousness of the divine to stay the baser passions of men, evil had no alternative but to turn upon and rend itself. This has been ever the case in the struggle of mankind to rise to greater and purer heights in its endeavor to escape from the bondage of materiality. Throughout the ages the advance of mankind has been accomplished through a long and tedious series of advancements and retrogressions.

Spiritual vision has raised the race gradually from the lowest type of human existence upward toward the high goal of holiness, but this has been accomplished only through footsteps and through the lessons gained from bitter experience. At first the faint gleams of spiritual existence found men at about the lowest ebb of materialism. Through the spiritual enlightenment which has been coming to them gradually down through the ages, men have been emerging steadily, although slowly, out of their cocoon of materialism. This advancement has come to them in proportion to the measure of true thought which they have admitted into consciousness.

There have been periods of spiritual growth which have lifted thought somewhat out of its materiality. The growth has brought with it a sense of material freedom and prosperity which men have allowed themselves to believe were the accomplishments of their own material efforts; and in time they have lost sight of the spiritual and have dropped back into their material ways, until they have been confronted with the fruits of their own backsliding. They have had to encounter war, calamity, plagues and disaster, until their lesson had been learned, and they were ready again to resume their pathway heavenward with the help and guidance of God gained through repentance, purification, humility and spiritual allegiance. On the occasion of each one of these experiences of retrogression and reform, men have gone a little higher in the scale of Spirit. They have advanced and dropped back, advanced and dropped back again, but each advancement has taken them a little higher than the previous one because of the higher lessons which have been learned. The race has arrived at its present stage of advancement, and now comes another period of human retrogression through which lessons must be learned and thought purged and purified.

Healing Is in Individual Consciousness

In *Science and Health* Mrs. Eddy says, "All that is material is a material, human, mortal thought, always governing itself erroneously," and in the same book she says, "Matter is neither self-existent nor a product of Spirit. An image of mortal thought, reflected on the retina, is all that the eye beholds." And again she says, "Bones have only the substance of thought which forms them." And in *Science and Health* we find this statement, "Mortal mind sees what it believes as certainly as it believes what it sees. It feels, hears and sees its own thoughts." Thus we find that our world exists in our own consciousness and is an object of our own individual creating. This brings out the complete individuality of existence. The concepts or objects of mortal mind are individual, and the only place healing can be accomplished either for ourselves or for others is in our individual consciousness. Inasmuch as the material world is a concept in individual consciousness, our work in Christian Science for the world and for humanity lies only in individual consciousness. You and I are not confronted with a world outside ourselves which needs to be healed. We are confronted with an individual concept of world which needs to be healed, and therefore our work for the healing of the world lies in our own thinking. As individual thought is purified, our individual world becomes purified, and this individual purification is what will bring a better world to all of us.

You may recall the question and answer in *Miscellaneous Writings* where we read this: "In your book, Science and Health, page 181, you say: 'Every sin is the author of itself, and every invalid the cause of his own sufferings.' On page 182 you say: 'Sickness is a growth of illusion, springing from a seed of thought — either your own thought or another's.' Will you please explain this seeming contradiction?"

In answer to the above, Mrs. Eddy gives us the following: "No person can accept another's belief, except it be with the consent of his own belief. If the error which knocks at the door of your own thought originated in another's mind, you are a free moral agent to reject or to accept this error; hence you are the arbiter of your own fate, and sin is the author of sin. In the words of our Master, you are a liar, and the father of it (the lie)."

From this we see that we do not have to accept into our world what others accept into their world, even though it might come in the form of universal belief. And thus we see how individual our world is, as well as our salvation from the world's claims of evil and materiality. So you and I can proceed right here and now to heal ourselves of the belief that evil has any power, source, channel or propulsion. In fact, we have got to recognize that error is "neither person, place nor thing," as Mrs. Eddy tells us, and in this way we deprive the claims of error of a channel through which to operate, because the only channel error has, is what you and I give it in thought. We have got to handle every world situation in an entirely impersonal manner and realize that the claim is no more real, personal, or powerful than a claim of smallpox or poverty. We cannot impersonalize evil by consciously giving it a personality to work through and then by hating that personality. If a patient with sickness comes to you for help, you could not heal that patient by hating him. You would have to love him before you could heal him. In *Science and Health* Mrs. Eddy writes, in speaking of the healing of the sick: "If the Scientist reaches his patient through divine Love, the healing work will be accomplished at one visit, and the disease will vanish into its native nothingness like dew before the morning sunshine." And so it is with our work in connection with world problems. We must free our thought of all sense of hate, resentment, and fear before we can hope to approach with any degree of success the problems which confront us.

The whole present day situation throughout the world is a chemicalization of what might be termed universal consciousness, and some individuals have allowed themselves to become mesmerized to the point where they have let the error in. It is a universal claim and must be handled as such; and inasmuch as you and I, as Christian Scientists, see it for what it is, and are the only ones in the whole world who understand and can apply the remedy, it is up to you and me to get busy and daily work on these problems which are of such vital importance not only to us, but to every human being.

Death

I received a letter from a student containing the following: "A discussion was occasioned by the article in *The Christian Science Journal* April, 1918, by Mrs. Eddy on 'Life.' In this article Mrs. Eddy says, 'No change has been wrought when we say my friend has just died; that friend is saying in the full consciousness of existence and with the same surroundings, 'I never died. It was but a dream I had. For life is going on with me the same as before. I am not spirit, yet I am as much flesh and bones as I ever was; the only change to me is, I cannot communicate with my friends — and why? Because they do not understand me now. They call me spirit, but I am not. They say I died, but I did not. They do not know what I am, where I am or what I am pursuing. I shall not be spirit until I lose all limits! They have lost their evidences of me through their personal senses, because they have said I changed, I died; their mistaken views of life have parted us; their belief that life ended with me, or took upon itself a new form, has prevented their understanding the reality of my present existence, hence our separation through these opposite beliefs and our opposite conditions as the result thereof. Further communication between us is impossible, until their belief changes through the footsteps that mine has done and become like mine. This change will be named death, but that is their belief of it, not ours who have rent the veil that hides the mystery of a moment.

"'Yes, we shall know each other there! We shall love and be loved; we shall never lose our identity, but find it more and more in its order, beauty and goodness.'"

The writer of the letter goes on to say that the gentleman with whom she had the discussion said that Mrs. Eddy never intended this to be printed. "He argues," she says, "that we are not conscious of the same material surroundings, same rugs, same books, same chairs but, if after the experience of death there is still need of these things we would have a different creation, but to believe that we would still be sitting in a green chair in the same room, would be to accept spiritualism."

Don't allow yourself to get into a panic or become doubtful every time some Christian Scientist makes statements which disagree with what you know to be true. Christian Science is not a matter of opinion or speculation. It is a Science. It is logical, and if one of the statements of Christian Science is true, all must be true. That is, if you take any fundamental truth in Christian Science and build up your conclusions and deductions on the basis of that statement, you cannot go wrong.

The article on " Life," by Mrs. Eddy is authentic, and whether or not Mrs. Eddy intended that it should appear in the

Journal is entirely beside the point. There are many things that Mrs. Eddy wrote which have not been printed, for many reasons. There are many things which Mrs. Eddy wrote which she did not want printed because she did not feel that the world, or the field, was ready for them. Whether or not the article on "Life" might be one of those articles I do not know, but there is no question about the authenticity of the article or the correctness of it, and because it might not agree with what someone thinks on the subject of death, is no good reason why its contents should not be considered as a correct guide for all Christian Scientists.

Furthermore, Mrs. Eddy has said no more in that article on "Life" concerning the phenomenon of death than she has said in many other places in her writings. And again, if what Mrs. Eddy says in the article on "Life," is not correct, then Mrs. Eddy's teaching as to the mental nature of matter is not correct. As I have said before, Science is not only scientific, but it is logical; and if one statement is true, there can be no mistake in conclusions based upon that statement even though our search takes us into the question of death. One cannot understand the truth about the condition of mortals after the experience called death until one understands what Christian Science teaches as to the mental nature of matter. If what Mrs. Eddy wrote on the subject of death in her article on "Life" is not correct, then what she has given us as to the mental nature of matter is not correct, and we might just as well quit and call it a day. There is no other conclusion to be reached than that outlined in "Life," if what she teaches as to matter is true.

In *Science and Health* we find the following: "'In the place where the tree falleth, there it shall be.' So we read in Ecclesiastes. This text has been transformed into the popular proverb, 'As the tree falls, so it must lie.' As man falleth asleep, so shall he awake. As death findeth mortal man, so shall he be after death, until probation and growth shall effect the needed change." Now, that is perfectly plain, and in effect is exactly what Mrs. Eddy says in the article on "Life." In the *Journal* of June 1886, there appeared an article by Mrs. Eddy in part as follows: "In no subject is there more interest than in the future life, and religious believers and leaders are often asked about it. One inquirer phrases her question in this way: 'After the change called death takes place, do we meet our friends who have gone before, or does life continue in thought only, as in a dream?'

"Man is not annihilated nor does he lose his identity by passing through the belief called death. After his momentary belief passes from the erring mortal mind, man finds himself still in a conscious state of existence. He learns that he has but passed through an extreme moment of mortal fear, to awaken with thoughts and being as material as before.

"Mental spiritualization is not attained by physical death but by a conscious union with God. When we are on the same plane of conscious existence with those gone before, we shall be able to communicate with them and recognize them. When we have done our work here so well that it needs not to be done over again, the death change increases our joys and our means of advancement."

In *Miscellaneous Writings*, in answer to the following question, "After the change called death takes place, do we meet those gone before? — or does life continue in thought only as a dream?" Mrs. Eddy writes: "Man is not annihilated, nor does he lose his identity by passing through the belief called death. After the momentary belief of dying passes from mortal mind, this mind is still in a conscious state of existence; and the individual has but passed through a moment of extreme mortal fear, to awaken with thoughts, and being as material as before. *Science and Health* clearly states that spiritualization of thought is not attained by the death of a body, but by a conscious union with God. When we shall have passed the ordeal called death, or destroyed this last enemy, and shall come upon the same plane of conscious existence with those gone before, then shall we be able to communicate with and to recognize them."

In *Science and Health* we find the following: "Mortals waken from the dream of death with bodies unseen by those who think that they bury the body." Mrs. Eddy has said and written many other things bearing on this subject, but the above are sufficient for our present needs.

The Mental Nature of Matter

All of the above quotations from Mrs. Eddy tie in together in one harmonious whole with her teaching regarding the mental nature of matter. Matter, we have learned, or should have learned, is but the objective state of our own material consciousness. What you and I see, feel, taste, smell and hear, is objectified consciousness, and that objectified consciousness is strictly and distinctly individual. It makes no difference how many people may see the same thing; it makes no difference how many people, for instance, may see this table at which I am sitting; as far as you are individually concerned, this table is the objectified state of your own individual consciousness. The only place this table exists, as far as you are concerned, is in your own consciousness. So you are not concerned as to what may be objectified in my consciousness, nor are you concerned as to what might be termed the objectified manifestation of universal thought or consciousness. In its last analysis, existence in all of its phases or varied manifestations, is individual. In *Retrospection and Introspection*, Mrs. Eddy says, "The lie (that is, matter) was, and is, collective as well as individual." By that she means that no matter what collective thinking may accomplish in the line of objectified error, or matter, it can have no bearing on individual existence until individual consciousness has accepted into thought the evidence of this collective or universal thinking; and then existence, or the consciousness of universal or collective thought, becomes strictly individual and loses its universal aspect. So in its last analysis whatever you and I behold in our universe is decidedly the objectified state of our own thinking, and therein, and therein only, does salvation become individual.

As I have explained before, if Jesus' so-called material existence, or world, had been the objectified manifestation of universal thought or collective thinking, Jesus never could have accomplished his ascension until every individual on earth had ceased thinking materially, and universal consciousness had become strictly and wholly spiritual. Because the body and the material world of Jesus existed only in his individual consciousness, and was not dependent on the thinking of others, Jesus was enabled to overcome the world and his body at the moment of his ascension, rather than being compelled to wait on the demonstration of others before he could enter heaven. The demonstration of Jesus at the time of his ascension proved for all time that existence is strictly individual and that the thinking of others has nothing to do with your and my individual worlds or with our demonstration over matter. We live in our own individual worlds, and these worlds are of our own creating. There are just as many worlds as there are people. Your material world is but the objectified manifestation of your own consciousness, and my material world is but the objectified manifestation of my own consciousness. Therefore, our bodies, our worlds, everything is individual.

How does all this tie in with an explanation of the experience of death? Why, in this way. Material existence being strictly individual and the objectified manifestation of individual consciousness, mortals can never, as Mrs. Eddy tells us so definitely, become unconscious of matter until thought is spiritualized. In the quotation above from *Miscellaneous Writings*, Mrs. Eddy says: "Science and Health clearly states that spiritualization of thought is not attained by the death of the body but by a conscious union with God." Therefore, if one's body is the objectified manifestation of his own state of consciousness, and if death does not change that consciousness, it must be perfectly obvious that we do not lose our concept of material body by passing through death.

Body — material body — occupies space only because of the human consciousness of matter. In Science there is no place, space, distance or location. Man exists in the infinitude of Mind. Therefore, matter seems to fill space or exist in space only because of thought. At the moment of Jesus' ascension his thought or consciousness became wholly spiritual; and when that wholly spiritual state of consciousness was accomplished, Jesus was without a material body. Space, place and localization are objects or illusions of the carnal mind just as is matter. Do away with the carnal in human consciousness and you do away with matter and place.

Therefore materially speaking, you and I consume space or fill place only in our individual consciousness. As matter is an individual concept, there are, as I said, just as many tables here as there are human minds to conceive it. Each of you holds this table in consciousness as a distinctly individual concept of individual consciousness. The same may be said of the human body. Your concept of your body is individual. My concept of your body exists only in my individual consciousness. Therefore, when a so-called body is buried, all that is placed in the ground is the concept of body which the individuals who have been left behind hold in consciousness; and the concept of body held by those who think they bury the body, is not the same concept of body as that held by the individual who is thought to be dead. To repeat Mrs. Eddy's quotation from *Science and Health*, "Mortals waken from the dream of death with bodies unseen by those who think that they bury the body."

Now, the reason that the body with which mortals awaken after death is unseen by those who think that they bury the body, is because those who bury the body think that the person who they are burying has died; whereas, as a matter of metaphysical fact, the person whom they think has died, has awakened from his dream of death with exactly the same material body he had before because his body exists in his consciousness only, and death has done nothing to his consciousness. In fact, if one accepts the belief of death, he has made that a part of his human consciousness. In *Science and Health*, Mrs. Eddy writes: "That Life is not contingent on bodily conditions is proved, when we learn that life and man [mortal man] survive this body. Neither evil, disease nor death can be spiritual, and the material belief in them disappears in the ratio of one's spiritual growth."

Quoting again from *Miscellaneous Writings*, Mrs. Eddy says, "After the momentary belief of dying passes from mortal mind, this mind is still in a conscious state of existence; and the individual has but passed through a moment of extreme fear, to awaken with thoughts, and being, as material as before." Now, if one awakens after death, "with thoughts and being as material as before" death, and if matter and body are the objectified manifestations of individual thought, can there be any other conclusion but that after the experience of death we are bound to have as our objectified existence, the same surroundings as before? If the object of my consciousness before death includes a material home, material surroundings, material furniture, etc. (and the only place these objects exist is in consciousness), could I possibly be conscious after death of any other house, any other furniture or any other surroundings? If you will follow your metaphysical reasoning right through from the explanation of matter in the experience of death, you will never become confused as to this explanation of the experience after death, and you will never be tempted to believe that Mrs. Eddy's explanation of death and its aftermath has anything in common with the belief of Spiritualism. In fact, the teachings of Christian Science as to death are not only the exact opposite of the teachings of Spiritualism, but they reveal the utter impossibility of Spiritualism and all it stands for.

The reason we are not conscious of those who have been left behind after the experience of death and the reason that those who have been left behind are not conscious of our material and bodily presence, is explained very clearly by Mrs. Eddy in the quotation from her article on "Life," as follows: "No change has been wrought when we say, 'My friend has just died.' That friend is saying in the full consciousness of existence (material existence) and with the same surroundings (material surroundings), 'I never died. It was but a dream I had. For life is going on with me the same as before. I am not spirit, yet I am as much flesh and bones as I ever was; the only change to me is I cannot communicate with my friends —and why? Because they do not understand me now. They call me spirit, but I am not. They say I died, but I did not. They do not know what I am, where I am or what I am pursuing. I shall not be spirit until I lose all limits. They have lost their evidence of me through their personal senses, because they have said I changed, I died. Their mistaken views of life have parted us. Their belief that life ended with me, or took upon itself a new form, has prevented their understanding the reality of my present existence, hence our separation through these opposite beliefs and our opposite conditions as a result thereof. Further communication between us is impossible, until their belief changes through the footsteps that mine has done and become like mine. This change will be named death, but that is their belief of it, not ours, who have rent the veil that hides the mystery of a moment.'"

Quite naturally, then, inasmuch as death does not change material existence in any way, after the experience called death, we shall most certainly be able to recognize and communicate materially, just as we do now with each other, with those friends who have gone before. There is no change materially simply through the experience of death, and Mrs. Eddy has explained very clearly in the above quotations the mental nature of the belief of separation between those who have gone and those who have been left behind. When the barrier of mental separation is broken through the experience of death, we shall find ourselves on material speaking terms and terms of recognition with those who have gone before just as naturally and materially as here.

The reason I say that when the mental barrier of separation has broken through the experience of death, there will be a union with those who have gone before, is because that is the only way we will be able, in our present state of advancement, to accomplish the union with the departed. If it were possible for you and me to make the demonstration over matter and body that Jesus made at the time of his ascension, we would have avoided the experience of death and would have become so spiritual and free from materiality that we could not recognize those who had gone before because our spirituality would have taken us beyond their material state of consciousness. In other words, through spiritual growth, we would be so far in advance of those who had accepted the argument of death in matter that we would not be able to recognize them nor they us.

One student asks in this connection, "In passing through the belief of death are mortals ever conscious of a grave. Must they demonstrate over the belief of grave?" No, my understanding is that when one passes on, one awakens in exactly the same location, position and with the same material surroundings and accompaniments that he is conscious of at the moment of death.

You see, matter is but a condition of thought; and if thought is changed about its own objectification, matter disappears in the consciousness of the one whose thought has been changed. In such an instance — in the explanation of the reason for the separation between the departed and those who have been left behind — we find that the material evidence of carnal thinking calling itself matter may be changed , in certain instances, without spiritualization of thought. That is, if we believe that another has died and the body has been buried, we are not spiritualizing thought in any way, for we do not see the physical evidence of the one who has died; we simply have changed our thought about him. We have not spiritualized thought about him. He has assumed in our consciousness a different state of existence because of our change of thought, and that different state of existence is just as material in our consciousness as the former state of existence.

The question as to whether we are conscious of the grave after death was based upon the statement in *Science and Health* as follows: "The lonely precincts of the tomb gave Jesus a refuge from his foes, a place in which to solve the great problem of being." It must be remembered that everything Jesus did, all of the experiences he underwent in his brief career on earth, were for the guidance and elevation of mankind. Mrs. Eddy tells us that he could have avoided all of the experiences which he underwent. However, to become the Wayshower and the Saviour, Jesus had to go through experiences which would prove to mortals the truth of what he had been teaching. He could have avoided the experience on the cross, but if it were not for that experience and what followed there would be no Christianity. He could have avoided the tomb, but to bring the lesson of life home to mankind, Jesus had to undergo the experience of the tomb. Men would not have understood if he had done otherwise. Then, again, it is more than likely that the experience of Jesus on the cross did not deprive him of his conscious state of existence. It is not possible to compare the experience of Jesus with those of mortals, because Jesus went through what he did merely as an example to us. At the time of the crucifixion, and even some time before that, Jesus was so close to the borderline between matter and Spirit that there is a marked blending which puts some of his experiences beyond the realm of the human.

When Jesus raised Lazarus from the tomb, Jesus had to effect Lazarus' reappearance in a manner that would be understandable to those who were there. Jesus had to effect Lazarus' reappearance in a body which his friends thought that they buried. Otherwise there would have been no lesson. Matter is but the objective state of mortal mind, and those who buried Lazarus could not see him in any state or body but that in which they buried him. Jesus' reappearance to his disciples after his resurrection, with the spear thrusts in his side and the nail prints in his hands, was the only form in which the disciples could be convinced that it was the selfsame Jesus. The disciples could only see what they held in consciousness; and as they buried Jesus with the bodily evidences of the crucifixion on him, they could not see him resurrected without those same evidences. Jesus did not have to appear to them with the spear thrusts in his side. It was the disciples own consciousness of Jesus that united his reappearance with the spear thrusts.

You and I see, feel, taste, smell and hear only what we hold in consciousness. There are, naturally, a great many questions which come to thought in connection with this question of death which can only be answered through experience, and, so far, I am not looking for that experience, so there are many questions which you might want answered in this regard which I am not now capable of answering.

Treatment

A treatment in Christian Science is the attainment in individual consciousness of the clear concept of man's unity with God. Every Christian Scientist should be able to do his own metaphysical work. Class instruction is for the purpose of equipping one with that understanding which will enable him to instantly meet, with the right spiritual conception, every challenge which the carnal or mortal mind might attempt to put in his way. Remember that the carnal mind is a creation of the human consciousness. God did not create the carnal mind; and as God is the only creator there is, there can be in reality no carnal or mortal mind. If there is no carnal or mortal mind, there is, then, no origin of evil, sin or sickness. The carnal mind, as Mrs. Eddy tells us, is simply an idol or creation of the human consciousness, and all that needs to be healed is the human consciousness of the belief that there is a carnal mind from which could emanate erroneous beliefs.

As I have so many times before explained, there is in reality no human consciousness any more than there is a carnal mind; but there is the claim of human consciousness from which every mortal must be free before he can enter into that state of conscious existence which we call heaven. The carnal mind, or the mortal mind, is an illusion of the human consciousness. In our work in

Christian Science we are not endeavoring to heal the human body, the carnal mind, or the mortal mind; we are endeavoring to heal the human consciousness, and that is all we are endeavoring to heal. The only place a human being seems to exist is in his human consciousness, not in the carnal mind or the mortal mind, and don't you let anyone tell you differently. If God did not create the carnal mind, there must be some explanation of its seeming existence before its baneful effects can be met and overcome.

One of the most prolific sources of freedom from the bondage of the carnal or mortal mind is the understanding that it is but a fabrication of the human consciousness. If this were not so, how would we be able to minimize and annul its effects? If any thing or any agency but the human consciousness were responsible for the existence of the carnal mind, there would be no possible prospect of individual salvation. Each individual consciousness creates its own individual world of matter, and that consciousness creates the agency through which that material world is manifested, as certainly as it creates its world. It is because of this fact that each one of us is enabled, here and now, to master the material through the influx into the human consciousness of the spiritual facts of being. The material exists only in individual human consciousness, and it is in individual human consciousness that the material must be overcome through the influx therein of divine ideas. If you and I were not the creator of the carnal mind by reason of which we live in matter, you and I could never heal the sick or save ourselves from the bondage of materialism. In *Science and Health* Mrs. Eddy tells us that "the human mind alone suffers and is sick." That's plain. She doesn't say anything about the carnal mind suffering or the mortal mind being sick. She says that the "human mind alone suffers and is sick." Hence, it must be the human mind that needs healing. And Mrs. Eddy says further, "It breaks the dream of disease to understand that sickness is formed by the human mind, not by matter nor by the divine Mind." As we know that matter and mortal mind are one, it is clear from this last quotation that sickness is not formed by mortal mind, but rather by the human consciousness, operating through the mortal or carnal mind of its own creating.

Now, I am not going again into a discussion of the human mind or human consciousness as we have so thoroughly and exhaustively canvassed that point many times before; but in considering the matter of treatment or practice, it is well to have in mind what Mrs. Eddy brings out in all her writings regarding the human mind and disease. The terms human mind and human consciousness are used interchangeably by Mrs. Eddy in most instances. The carnal mind cannot be healed and the divine Mind does not need to be healed. All that needs healing is the human consciousness of the belief of a carnal mind outside itself. When the human mind is healed of its belief in a mortal or carnal mind capable of inducing sickness, inharmony, misery, sorrow and the like, then will sickness, poverty, inharmony cease to be a part of individual experience. As the human consciousness takes to itself carnal or mortal thoughts, these thoughts, in turn, become objectified or externalized as matter, sickness, poverty, and discord. As Mrs. Eddy has expressed it in *Science and Health*, "The fading forms of matter, the mortal body and the material earth, are the fleeting concepts of the human mind." Matter does not exist outside the human consciousness. The carnal mind does not exist as matter until it is admitted to the human consciousness. Matter exists only as a false belief, and a false belief must have a believer. The believer is the human consciousness.

From this it is evident that all material phenomena exists only in the individual human consciousness. You are asked to do some work in Christian Science for someone who thinks he lives a thousand miles away from you. Without any reference to the absolute statement concerning the situation, or without any reference to a statement of the situation existing between you and your patient in the absolute, where does this patient exist as far as you are physically concerned? Where does a man who claims to be a thousand miles away from you exist materially? Does he exist any where but in your own individual consciousness? No. It does not make any difference what mortal mind says about distances, space, localization, material form, outline or shape, the fact is that all material objectification or manifestation exists only in individual consciousness. Time and place, location, space and distance do not exist materially or as material phenomena. They exist only in individual consciousness, and you and I cannot get away from individual consciousness. So an individual who claims to be a thousand miles away from you and who calls or writes you for help in Christian Science, is no farther away from you, as a matter of metaphysical fact, than your consciousness, and you know that you and your consciousness are one. Therefore, where does an absent treatment come in? It doesn't come in. It isn't. There is no absent treatment. In *Science and Health* Mrs. Eddy says, "It is no more difficult to read the absent mind than it is to read the present," and "Science can heal the sick who are absent from their healers, as well as those present, since space is no obstacle to Mind."

Nowhere in her writings does Mrs. Eddy speak of "absent treatment." She says that Science can heal those who are absent from their healers, but that is the only mention she makes to what might be called an absent treatment.

Now, approaching the situation from the standpoint of man in God's image and likeness, and that is the standpoint you will have to take at all times in giving a treatment, man is infinite — he is just as infinite as his Maker if he is the image of his Maker. Man, generic man, is one; and that one man, which fills infinity, is the man which must be the basis of your treatment. It is the truth about the man of God's creating that you have to know to heal the sick. As I have said, there is no truth about a mortal man, a sick man, or a localized or limited man. Man must be just as big as God; and to the extent that you can mentally apprehend this real man and his indissoluble connection with the Father Mind, to that extent will your work become instantly effective. We read in Proverbs, "Where there is no vision, the people perish." It is the true vision or concept of God and man in individual consciousness that heals, and the closer we live to God, the surer and more constant this vision, so that healing becomes spontaneous and instantaneous in the proportion that thought remains fixed on the supernal.

God is infinite Mind, or divine consciousness, and man is the consciousness of the divine expressed. Therefore, God and man are inseparable, and the truth about God is the truth about man. There is not anything true about God that is not true about man if man is image; and there can be no separation between God and man if God is consciousness, or Mind, and man is idea, or consciousness expressed. Therefore, if man is just as ever present as God, there is no absent man, and the truth about the man that God creates is the truth about man ever present; therefore, man is ever present and there can be no absent man about which the truth is known. If you were called upon to help a man who claimed to be a thousand miles away from you, the truth about the ever-present man of God is the only truth you would know. You would not try to heal a localized material organization calling itself man located a thousand miles away from you. You wouldn't give mortal mind enough consideration to waste any time on trying to know the truth about such a man. There isn't any truth about such a man. You would devote your time to knowing the truth about that ever present infinite expression of God which is right here and now. This realization in consciousness does away entirely with the argument of distance, time, space, place and separation without needing any denial of these arguments of mortal mind. Your very consciousness of the infinitude and the eternal presence of man in God's image and likeness would, in itself, meet and handle the arguments of distance, space and separation.

All there is in infinity is God and man, and God and man are just as inseparable as is the sun's rays from the sun. God is divine consciousness, and the expression of that consciousness is man. The expression of that divine consciousness does not originate or have its inception in man. Expression lies in God. God creates man. Man does not create himself. The consciousness which constitutes man is God bestowed, and the consciousness which constitutes man constitutes man's universe. The brotherhood of man does not lie in man; it lies in God, because man is God's manifestation, and man has no inspiration, intuition, or impulse which is not from God. Man has no mind of his own, no will of his own and no volition of his own. Man is God manifested, or God manifesting Himself. Man doesn't manifest man. God manifests man. Therefore, man is God's responsibility and not man's. The love which you and I reflect in consciousness comes from the same source, and that source, or Mind, never relinquishes the love which you and I reflect.

The love which you and I reflect remains in God eternally, and thus is the brotherhood of man maintained and sustained in Mind throughout eternity. Speaking materially, man's consciousness constitutes man's world. The material world is simply the externalized expression of the carnal in consciousness. Mrs. Eddy tells us that matter and mortal mind are one. Therefore, when you and I behold a material object, we are looking at mortal mind, or, in other words, we are seeing with mortal mind. We see what we hold in consciousness and what we see is not something extraneous to ourselves. What we see is our own selves. We can't become conscious through any of the five physical senses of anything we do not hold in thought. Our world will hold no love for us if thought is filled with hate. Our world will hold no abundance for us if thought is filled with human limitations and inhibitions. Our world will hold no joy for us if thought is filled with sorrow. Our world will hold no harmony for us if thought is filled with rancor, unrest and indecision. Our world will hold no justice for us if thought is filled with injustice. Mrs. Eddy tells us, "Divine Love always has met and always will meet every human need," and yet on all sides we find ourselves confronted with human need, want and distress. Where does this human need, want and distress exist? Why has not divine Love met that human need?

In answer to the first query as to human need, want, distress, the only place human need, or any material manifestation for that matter, exists is in individual human consciousness. The need does not exist in matter or in person. It exists in individual human consciousness. The only reason you and I can see another person in need of anything is because of the need in our own consciousness. So human need exists in individual consciousness, and it is the human consciousness that must be healed of the human need, and not matter or person. Now, what is it that is going to heal that human need which exists only in individual human consciousness? Why, nothing but divine Love. And why has not divine Love already met that human need which you and I see all about us? Simply because *our individual consciousness is not been filled with divine Love.* If the human need exists in individual human consciousness, it is divine Love in individual human consciousness that is necessary to heal the human need. So as existence is individual, salvation is individual, and there is nothing vicarious about salvation. There are no short cuts, and no one else can take our footsteps for us. If you believe that twice two is five, the fact that someone else might know that twice two is four would not help you. You have got to know the truth for yourself.

There are many things I would like to take up with you today, but I shall have to close. Perhaps I shall someday learn to finish my remarks within a reasonable time. Before closing, however, let me give you a few brief statements to take with you:

> Remember that your concept of God constitutes your God;
> that man is as infinite as God and as pure and holy as God;
> that man is not materially outlined, formed or shaped;
> that man does not fill space or exist in place — he is consciousness;

that man does not include — he reflects;
that man does not contain — he expresses;
that man is an involuntary expression of God and cannot help but be as perfect as his Maker;
that man is God's responsibility and is himself under no individual responsibility, liability or obligation;
that God manifests Himself as man;
that God maintains His own reflection in infinity and throughout eternity;
that man's individuality and identity remain eternally in Mind, and that man is inspired, animated, governed and controlled by God;
that man includes his universe and that man and his universe are one;
that Life includes man — man does not include Life.

THE PRACTICE OF CHRISTIAN SCIENCE

Association Address of 1928

I want to take up again that phase of metaphysics — the fact that each one of us lives in a world of his own creating. Probably one of the most concise statements appearing of late along that line, outside of the writings of Mrs. Eddy, was the statement I read from the pen of a noted English physical scientist, quoted as follows: "Of the intrinsic nature of matter, science knows nothing and never can know anything. Science tells us nothing as to what matter is. For all we know, matter may itself be mental. The old view, therefore, that atoms or electrons are the ultimate reality, and that, by interacting on one another in accordance with the laws of nature, they produce our minds with all their hopes and aspirations, has no longer any scientific basis. Another bugbear that many artists and religious people have found so depressing, the iron laws of nature, also acquire an entirely new status as the result of recent scientific work. It can be shown that these laws are the results of the mind's own action. The laws of nature are not something imposed on an independently existing universe from without. Indeed, not only the laws of nature, but space and time and the material universe itself, are constructions of the human mind. To an altogether unsuspected extent the universe we live in is a creation of our own minds."

And there it is in a nut shell. Everything we see, feel, taste, hear, or smell we see, feel, taste, hear, smell by mortal consciousness, and not by any of the organs of seeing, feeling, tasting, smelling or hearing. We are born into the world as infants without any of our faculties of sense developed to any extent. We come into the world seeing, feeling, tasting, smelling and hearing as a result of the thinking of our mental parents. We are not cognizant of anything, or scarcely anything, that a mortal is cognizant of. We know neither good nor bad. Our growth and our maturity are the outward evidences of the accretion of mortal beliefs solely. We grow by taking on mortal mind, mortal beliefs, mortal thoughts, and as we take on these thoughts, then our world begins to shape itself in our consciousness so that each individual consciousness constitutes the world of each individual. We each see materially what each one holds in consciousness.

The reason that you and I may see or become cognizant of the same material thing, is not because of the thing, but because we both are entertaining the same sense of human belief about things. The material world is not an entity existing in and of itself independent of our individual thinking. It is a product of our thinking. And as our thinking is rid of materiality, then our world is rid of materiality. As our thinking takes on materiality, our world takes on materiality. In the book of Proverbs it is written, "As a man thinketh in his heart so is he." That is, of course, according to the consciousness each individual entertains, so will his world be. So do you not see how we can make our own environment good or bad, according to our own state of consciousness? No one outside of ourselves has anything to do with the material world that we think surrounds us, because there is nothing outside of one's own consciousness that one can be cognizant of. Mrs. Eddy has expressed the same thought as the one just quoted from Proverbs where she says in *Science and Health*, "Beauty, as well as truth, is eternal; but the beauty of material things passes away, fading and fleeting as mortal belief. Custom, education, and fashion form the transient standards of mortals. . . . It is Love which paints the petal with myriad hues, glances in the warm sunbeam, arches the cloud with the bow of beauty, blazons the night with starry gems, and covers earth with loveliness."

We all know, as Christian Scientists, that God, or Love, knows nothing about the material petal of the rose, the rays of sun, the rainbow, the stars or the earth, and yet Mrs. Eddy here tells us that it is Love (God) which paints the petal with myriad hues. It appears on the face of things as a contradiction; but in the light of the fact that we make our own world, our own environment, it becomes clear that the more of Love we hold in consciousness, the more of God we reflect in our thinking, the more Godlike the material things become to us. It is certain that the petal of a flower would not appear to a hating thought with the same beauty and promise that it would appear to a person whose thoughts were filled with love. It is the love in our own thinking that makes things beautiful to us. To a thorough materialist, to one steeped in crime and degradation, nothing much is very lovely or promising. One whose consciousness was not reflecting love would not find much beauty in the sun, the moon, the stars, or the flowers. So as we fill our thinking with that Love which is God, then we are seeing nothing but loveliness in the world about us. That is, we are making our own environment one of loveliness by our own thinking.

Matter Reduced to Thought Alone

And so with the claims of sickness. We relieve matter of all its danger and harm and bad effects by correcting the thought which endows matter with evil influence with the right thought — the true thought about the thing before us. Inasmuch as the world in which you and I live is a product of our own consciousness or thinking, it can readily be seen how we can bring happiness and beauty into the world, not by changing the world, or by changing people, but by filling our thoughts so full of love and truth that evil and unhappiness will not come into our experience. Remember this, and you may save yourselves and others a great deal of unhappiness and pain — that the moment the actions, the activities or the attitude of another begins to give you concern, then is the time for you to get busy with your own mental household, and do a little house-cleaning on your own account.

The actions, attitude or activities of others will not concern or bother you unless your own consciousness is all wrong. You cannot make the world a nice place to live in, nor can you make conditions about you tolerable, simply by changing material conditions or people. Material conditions and people please or annoy you in proportion as your own thought is right or wrong. We see, feel, taste, smell and hear just exactly what we think. Just the moment you and I cease our thinking, just that moment does the material disappear. Matter exists only in thought. It has no substance nor entity not given it by mortal thinking. Remember, in this connection, that Mrs. Eddy says in *Science and Health*, "Metaphysics resolves *things* into *thoughts*, and exchanges the objects of sense for the ideas of Soul." And in *Miscellaneous Writings*, she writes: "Midst the falling leaves of old-time faiths, above the frozen crust of creed and dogma, the divine Mind-force, filling all space and having all power, upheaves the earth. In sacred solitude divine Science evolved nature as thought, and thought as things."

Therefore, the thought of the thing is the thing. The only thing that makes matter tangible to you and me is the thought we entertain about it. It does not exist outside of human consciousness. So when each individual human consciousness is bereft of its material thinking by the substitution of right thinking, then matter disappears and the demonstrations of Jesus become possible to all of us. If the walls of the room in which the eleven disciples were gathered after Jesus' crucifixion and burial in the tomb, did not exist simply as creations of thought, Jesus never could have appeared in their midst when the doors were all closed and the windows bolted. If distance and time and space had appeared to Jesus in any other form than thought, he could not have instantaneously transported the ship across the Sea of Galilee. On that occasion, he entered the ship with his disciples and immediately the ship was on the other side without the passage of time or the operation of material motion or effort on the part of Jesus or those with him.

As I have repeatedly pointed out, we must guard our conception of the metaphysical translation of matter, and watch that we do not get the erroneous impression that many seem to have — that when we have resolved matter into thought, we have spiritualized matter, and gotten the spiritual truth back of that which calls itself matter. We have not spiritualized matter by resolving matter into thought, and we have not begun to get at the spiritual fact concerning which matter is the lie. We have simply taken the mask off of matter and seen it for what it is. Matter is thought, and there is no more spirituality in the thought, than there is in the matter because matter is thought. They are not two; they are one and the same thing. So in resolving things into thoughts, do not become confused with the suggestion that the thought back of the material thing is the spiritual fact about the thing. The fact about matter is that, inasmuch as it is a figment of thought or mortal mind, and inasmuch as there is in reality, as Mrs. Eddy says in *Science and Health*, "No mortal mind out of which to make material beliefs, springing from illusion," there is, therefore, no matter; and in treating disease, that fact must be perfectly clear in our thinking — that there is no matter and hence no material condition to be met or cured.

In translating material things in their native element, mortal mind or thought, we have simply unmasked matter, and we see it for what it is — nothing. If matter exists as substance instead of thought, we never could heal it by right thinking. It is because matter and its accompaniments exist as wrong thought that we are able to bring a material change by right thinking. Matter and its sicknesses are simply our thoughts, our mortal thoughts externalized to our human consciousness; and therefore, if our thinking is changed, the objects of our thoughts must change to correspond to our thinking. If mortal thought tells us there is a sick man before us, and our understanding of Truth changes our thinking about that, then the object of our thoughts changes accordingly.

If mortal thought tries to bring us a sick man to heal, and our thought is so clear that a sick man does not exist in our thinking, then that which has claimed to be a sick man will respond to our correct view, and we behold a well man. God never made a sick man; therefore, the only reality a sick man has is what we give it in thought. So we see that when Christian Science resolves things into thoughts, it has not spiritualized things at all; it has simply removed the mask and matter appears for just what it is. But that is not where Mrs. Eddy leaves the situation. She does not say that "metaphysics resolves things into thoughts" and then leave it there, because no particular good would come from simply knowing what matter is. There must be a remedy. When we have resolved a thing into a thought, what then? Are we in any better position to cope with the situation? Is a thought less real than the thing itself when one realizes that the thing is a thought? No. Mrs. Eddy then goes on to give us the remedy. She says, "Metaphysics resolves things into thoughts and exchanges the objects of sense [which is the thing or the thought] for the ideas of Soul." Note that she does not say that the objects of sense or matter is changed into ideas of Soul. She says that these objects of sense, or thought, are *exchanged* for the ideas of Soul. That is, instead of changing matter into Spirit, or into the spiritual, we exchange the thought which claims to be matter by putting in its place a spiritual idea or spiritual ideas. So in reality, the translation of the material universe into the spiritual reality does not mean that we are changing mentally the material into the spiritual. It means that we are replacing the material with the spiritual.

And how is this done? Has God created two universes, one the material and the other the spiritual? Has God created the spiritual universe as real and the material universe as unreal? Has God ever created anything that would interfere with or change His vast spiritual universe of ideas? The answer to all of these questions is an obvious *no!* Then what do we do in making this change from the material to the spiritual? Why, the process is simply to become so clear in our understanding of the nothingness of matter that we can see, mentally, that all is, as Mrs. Eddy puts it in the

Scientific Statement of Being, "infinite Mind and its infinite manifestation." There is no matter and there is no mortal mind. Therefore, we do not treat matter, and we do not treat mortal mind. We put in their place ideas of divine Mind, or Soul, and thus we have our patient and all that claims to be the matter with him completely removed from the picture of matter, and in his place we have God's creation, perfect, spiritual and eternal.

Applying the Truth

And right in this connection I want to take up another phase of the work which seems to confuse many, although they do not seem to know it. So many people come to me and say that they can understand perfectly what is said about spiritual man and his perfection; but they do not see how to apply that to this so-called material man in a way that will heal him. Now, that is a very natural question, and it is, I am sure, quite a universal quandary among Scientists in general. It is, furthermore, a point upon which everyone of us must be clear before we can do a great deal along the line of healing. The trouble with most of us in our metaphysical work, is that we are endeavoring to heal a sick man. We are trying to make a metaphysical fact fit a physical mistake. We are trying to correct matter with Spirit. We are seeing man as two instead of one. We are seeing man as spiritual and, at the same time, in a state of error which needs to be corrected with the truth. Now understand this: You cannot apply a metaphysical fact to a physical error. That is, you cannot correct that which does not exist by the application of Spirit. Metaphysics does not really correct. It supplants. Is there any matter? Is there any sick matter? Is there a material man? Is there any materially sick man? Is there a mind which argues that there is matter, or material man, or sickness? To these questions also there is but one answer. An imperative *no!*

If there is any matter, material man, sickness, then you must give up the idea that God and His spiritual creation are omnipotent. If there are no such things as matter, material man, or sickness, what then is there to heal? Nothing. Absolutely nothing! You cannot make metaphysics relative. That is, there is no relative condition existing in Science. There is not a so-called materially sick man who needs to be healed. Get clear in your thought that in any condition, under any circumstance, with any problem of mortal mind, there is but one thing worthy of consideration and that is the absolute, the perfect, the spiritual.

The only answer to the question as to how one is to make the spiritual fact fit the material lie is that there is no material lie. The only truth about a lie is that it is not true, does not exist, has no existence. Then why try to heal that which does not exist? Why try to treat a man for a cancer when the only way to heal him is to understand clearly that there is no man with a cancer to be healed? Why try to heal a man of poverty, lack, failure, when there is no man who lacks, or has failed, or even made a mistake? If you admit, for an instant that man can be sick, that man (your patient, yourself) lives in matter or a material body, that he can be sick, or that he ever failed or made a mistake, then you have given the claim of error a past — a history, a place, or a condition from which it could have its origin — and you have them something that cannot be healed.

If a man comes to you to be healed of a condition which was the result of sin, would you attempt to heal that man by admitting that he had ever sinned? No, you would know that he never fell from his high estate as a Son of God. That there are not two of him, one the spiritual and the perfect child of God and the other the belief of a material man which could sin. You would know that the only reality there is, is man in the image and likeness of God, pure, holy, upright and eternal. You would know that that patient never fell from his high estate, and that he has never been thrust out of Spirit into matter, and that he has never been in any material condition, never been in any place or position in which God did not place him. Never fell, never sinned, never was anything less than an eternal expression of his Maker. You would see him as idea, as reflection, as expression of Mind, through idea, inseparable from the Mind that created him, and as such he could never express or image forth that which did not come from his Creator. You would know that because he had never been anything less than God's perfect expression through idea, and that because he never was in the environment or influence of any but the one perfect Mind, or Creator, he never sinned, and that therefore he cannot suffer for that which he never did. What is it that says that a man can sin, or suffer, or be wicked, or poverty stricken? Certainly not God, who fills all space, and knows nothing about such things. It must be mortal mind. And what is mortal mind? Does it exist? Has it a creator? Can it create?

If you were confronted with the argument of a man with a disease as a result of heredity, how would you handle it? Would you handle it by admitting that that man had been born of a material parent? That he had passed through the experience of birth? That he had ever had a prenatal existence? That he had ever had a material father, or mother, or grandfather, or grandmother? No, you would know that man, even that patient, was never in a material body; that he was never born into matter; that he never passed through a prenatal state; that he never was thrust out of Spirit; that he never had a material father, mother, or ancestor from whom he could inherit disease. You would see him not as a poor mortal with a disease to be healed, but as a child of God, free from disease. You would know that he was never born; that he never passed through a prenatal state; that he has no material father, mother, or ancestor. You would know that he was never born because he exists in divine consciousness as a perfect child of that consciousness, and that he is co-eternal and co-existent with God, without beginning and without ending. You would know that his father and mother is God, and that therefore he can inherit only good because only good exists in divine consciousness, his home. You would know that matter can neither feel, taste, smell, hear, nor create; that matter has no power to recreate or procreate; that matter cannot create, transmit or receive impressions or conditions because it has neither Mind, Principle, nor God. You would know that because man has his existence in God and always has had his existence in God, that this patient has never been in any position, condition, or experience where any of the beliefs of animal magnetism could be fastened on him through the argument of heredity; that no belief of heredity could fasten upon him any of the beliefs of family or racial characteristics, either of mind or body, because the only Mind there is, is God, and the only body there is, is the body of Christ. Man can inherit only that which exists, and nothing exists outside divine consciousness. Man cannot inherit that which has never been created. Man's father and mother being God, man's home is in divine Mind, or consciousness, and his family consists of ideas of that Mind which are all governed in perfect harmony by this all-seeing, all-acting, all-loving Mind. You would not admit in your thought for a moment any suggestion that this patient has inherited something terrible from a material parent.

Suppose you were confronted with a case of a person who was out of a position, or whose business was in bad shape, or who needed financial recuperation. Would you admit that that man was a material object who had been born into matter, and who had thus brought into the world a lot of ancestral traits of failure, and so on, with him? Would you admit that that man had ever been in a place, or position, or environment, that God had not placed him in? Would you admit that he was ever in a material business, or that he needed material money, or goods, or chattels? Would you admit that there was a condition of lack which needed to be handled? Would you admit that man can lack or need anything? No, to all of these questions.

You would immediately see that man to be a child of God, a compound expression of all the ideas of Mind, dwelling in the divine consciousness as a perfect child of Mind, and held in perfect place and position by the Mind that created him. You would know that man is idea, that he is the compound idea of Mind, reflecting all ideas, and that therefore he could not lack, or be limited, or out of place or position or right environment. You would know that every idea of Mind is here and now manifested through and to this patient, and that there is not one single idea lacking, and that every idea is held in perfect place and position by the Mind that created it, and that the ideas of Mind cannot be spent, impoverished, or lacking, because Mind cannot be exhausted, or spent, or lacking.

Man is idea and idea is infinite, filling all space, and in countless and infinite numbers, and these ideas cannot be depleted, or exhausted, or wasted away. You would know that, as a child of God, this patient is here and now the full and complete expression of Mind, and that he is inseparable from that Mind because an idea cannot be separated from the Mind that creates it. You would know that there are not two creations, and that therefore there are not two patients. You would know that there is but one, the perfect child of God, and that a child of God cannot be separated from his Creator because there is no extraneous or outside creation; there are not two creations, the material and the spiritual, but the one perfect creation.

You would know that, because of this fact, there is nothing that could possibly intervene between God and man, Creator and the created, to defile or defame. You would know that, because of this indissoluble connection between God and man, that this patient is therefore now in his right place, and expressing all the abundance and activity of Mind — all the abundance and activity there is. You would know that, because he is in his right place as a child of God, there is no influence or condition that could misplace him or put him in any place where God has not put him, and that because he is in his right place, he is here and now about his Father's business, and that therefore his business is good and profitable, and not subject to any of the laws of mortal mind. You would know that there is nothing outside illimitable divinity, and that therefore there are no laws of economy, hard times, fear, heredity, or what not, that can reach or find this expression of divine Mind; that he lives, moves and has his being in divine consciousness, and that because he is image and obedient to the Mind that created him, his business is expressing abundance, substance, right adjustment, peace, and joy. You would know, therefore, that because his business is expressing God, it is God-governed, God-managed, God-sustained, God-directed, God-supplied, and God-ordained.

You would not give any consideration to the argument that he might be in the clothing business, or the grocery business or the banking business. You would so remove him, in thought, from these environments and influences, that none of the limitations and arguments of failure with which these various human businesses are constantly threatened, could reach him. You would see him so removed from the human or mortal, and so entrenched in Mind as idea and child of God, that you could clearly see him as absolutely free from any of the so-called environments of human business. When you had your patient safely dwelling in divine Mind as a perfect child of Mind, you could then free him from any of the arguments of hard times, failure, lack, limitation, and human economic laws.

Mortal man and mortal conditions, you must remember, claim to exist as a result of some law, either broken or kept; and you must so unsee the material that no possibility of a law of matter will exist in your consciousness. Many men are called failures because failure seemed to be the law which governed their father and grandfather. You have to break that belief of the law of heredity by getting your patient into Mind and out of matter; and then as a child of God, you can see him as subject to only one law. There can't possibly be two sets of laws warring against each other. God never created one law to govern spiritual man and another law to govern material man. Nor did He create anything that could create laws governing material man. Material man and matter do not exist. Therefore they have no law. Error then has no God, no Principle, no law of origin, no law of existence, no law of expression or continuity. It does not exist. Break the claim of law to govern all material conditions by the understanding that matter has no mind or sensation, and that mortal mind does not exist. Therefore there is no material law to be broken. The only law there is, is the law of God, the law of perfection, of Spirit and Truth.

As I have stated, the basic error in the work of Christian Scientists, if there is something that seems to becloud or delay a healing, is that we do not rid thought of the belief that there are two of us — one the spiritual and one the material. If you will learn to confine your statements of Truth, your mental arguments concerning the patient, solely to statements of fact regarding the real, spiritual perfect man, and can see clearly that there is no material man to be healed, then you will not be working in the relative, but in the absolute.

The Mortal Dream

In *Science and Health* Mrs. Eddy has written: "Mortal existence is a dream of pain and pleasure in matter, a dream of sin, sickness, and death; and it is like the dream we have in sleep, in which everyone recognizes his condition to be wholly a state of mind. In both the waking and the sleeping dream, the dreamer thinks that his body is material and the suffering is in that body." She also says: "Mortal body and mind are one, and that one is called man; but a mortal isn't man, for man is immortal. A mortal may be weary or pained, enjoy or suffer, according to the dream he entertains in sleep. When that dream vanishes, the mortal finds himself experiencing none of these dream-sensations. To the observer, the body lies listless, undisturbed, and sensationless, and the mind seems to be absent. . . Now I ask, Is there any more reality in the waking dream of mortal existence than in the sleeping dream? There cannot be, since whatever appears to be a mortal man is a mortal dream. Take away the mortal mind, and matter has no more sense as a man than it has as a tree."

She also writes in the textbook: "Mortals are no more material in their waking hours than when they act, walk, see, hear, enjoy, or suffer in dreams. We can never treat mortal mind and matter separately, because they combine as one."

It is mortal mind, then, that moves the body and is back of the five physical senses. We go to sleep and we dream. What do we do in that dream? We may go from where we are, to sense, a thousand or ten thousand miles away. We see things materially just as certainly and just as positively as we do when we are awake. We feel the sensations of pain or pleasure as certainly when we are asleep as we do when we are awake, and those sensations of pain and pleasure in the body may be real to us a thousand miles away from where mortal mind says we went to sleep. We see, feel, taste, smell and hear as positively and as consciously in our sleep as we do when awake, and all the time we have the same body with us as certainly one time as another.

What then constitutes the mortal body with its five physical senses of seeing, feeling, tasting, smelling and hearing? Why simply human or mortal thinking. The body is no more real to us here and now than it is when we are asleep. So what is mortal body? Simply thought. What is a sick mortal body? Two mortal thoughts. Is there, then, any substance in what is termed matter? Certainly not. Then is there any mortal man to be sick, or suffer, or be poverty-stricken? Why then try to treat that which does not exist? Why try to treat a sick man, a mortal man, a poverty-stricken man, a man who calls himself a failure, if no such thing exists? And isn't the fact that no such thing exists, your only hope for salvation from these claims of so-called mortal existence? You cannot heal a sick man because there is no sick man to heal. And that is why, as I say, it is positively necessary, before we can make any headway in the healing work in Christian Science to get rid of the belief that there are two of us, and to become perfectly clear that there is but the one perfect creation right here and now.

And so in giving a treatment in Christian Science, does it make any difference if you confine your statements of truth to man, or to you, or to John Smith? That is, does the fact that you use in your treatment the term you, or John Smith, in directing your treatment, that you must become confused, or that the use of such terms admits the relative of a material you or a material John Smith? No matter what mortal mind may call itself, be it John Smith or Bill Jones, does that alter the fact in your thinking that the patient is a perfect spiritual creation of God dwelling in consciousness, divine consciousness, as idea, and that there is no material man or material thing to be healed? If you cannot, in your treatment, use the term man, or you, or John Smith, interchangeably, without becoming confused, then you have not become clear as to the nothingness of John Smith, as a material man. Mortal mind may call its concept of man, John Smith, but that does not alter the fact that what mortal mind calls John Smith does not exist, and that the individuality of what mortal mind calls John Smith dwells eternally and spiritually in the bosom of the Father, in divine Mind as idea. Mortal mind terms should not confuse our metaphysics or our sense of metaphysics.

Acknowledging Our Perfection

The question is sometimes asked as to whether or not we should claim for ourselves the perfection of man in the image and likeness of God here and now. It was asked if it would be erroneous to say that "right now I am a perfect, spiritual child of God." It was stated then that a student, a class taught student in Christian Science, had made the assertion that one should not claim perfection while in this state of so-called material existence. I presume that no one had ever been taught that, and that there was some confusion or misunderstanding somewhere in the mind of that student in regard to what he or she had been taught. Certainly no one with a grain of understanding of Christian Science could conceive for a moment that any treatment would ever accomplish anything along the line of healing that did not claim absolutely that right here and now is this patient a perfect, spiritual child of God, dwelling in divine consciousness as an idea in Mind, perfect, spiritual and eternal. Is there any matter? Is there any material man? If there is not, then what have we left? Why, nothing but perfect spiritual creation, perfect God and perfect man.

Mrs. Eddy tells us in *Science and Health*, "The Christlike understanding of scientific being and divine healing includes a perfect Principle and idea — perfect God and perfect man — as the basis of thought and demonstration." So you could not possibly proceed to treat a patient from any basis but that of his perfection — not his perfectibility, but his perfection. Upon what premise could you base a treatment in Christian Science if it is not the premise of perfection? Could you make one single declaration of truth about a patient unless it were based on the perfection of that patient as a child of God? On what basis could we deny error except on the basis that error does not exist? Can you take a relative position in Christian Science treatment and expect to heal the sick? Can you make your treatment scientific on the basis of two, one perfect and one imperfect individual joined together in some mysterious way? Now, the only fact about any man is that he is right now a perfect child of God, dwelling eternally in divine Mind, inseparable from that Mind. He has never been out of Mind and is not conscious of anything that does not come from that Mind. In *The People's Idea of God* Mrs. Eddy writes: "Even the pangs of death disappear, accordingly as the understanding that we are spiritual beings here reappears, and we learn our capabilities for good, which insures man's continuance and is the true glory of immortality."

So we see that it is only in proportion to our ability to see ourselves and our patients as perfect spiritual beings here and now, and thus to claim their divine birthright, that we are able to heal the sick and the sinning. Do not let the duality of mortal mind confuse you. Stick, in your statements, to the truth about God and His man, and that is all you need to do. Jesus said, "Ye shall know the truth and the truth shall make you free." Is there any truth about matter or mortal man? None in the least. Then the truth that Jesus referred to in that statement is the truth about the real man. And that is the only truth there is, and the only truth you and I need to know. There is no truth about sickness or a sick man.

Generic Man and Individual Man Defined

Now, in your work in Christian Science, do not make the very common mistake of spiritualizing things, and do not become confused concerning the spiritual idea. In Christian Science, we learn that all there is in God's kingdom is God and His creation. We learn that God is the parent Mind, or the only creative Principle of the universe, and that the universe of God's creating is spiritual — that is, it is idea. The only method Mind would ever have of expressing itself would be through idea. Mind could not be expressed in matter, mortal mind, or physical form. The only expression of God is idea, and the ideas of Mind go to make up God's universe, including man. Man, then, is a compound expression of all right ideas. There is no matter in an idea; therefore all of the ideas which go to make up the man of God's creating could not possibly be expressed in matter or anything material. Man, as a compound idea (and the thought of this compound idea seems to be confusing to some), is the full and complete expression of Mind and includes all creation. This full and complete expression of all the ideas of Mind constitute what Mrs. Eddy has termed generic man. In the textbook she has written, under the question "What is man?" the following: "Man is idea, the image, of Love; he is not physique. He is the compound idea of God, including all right ideas; the generic term for all that reflects God's image and likeness."

Thus we see that generic man includes all the ideas of Mind. Man, reflecting all the ideas of Mind, must include all the ideas of Mind which go to make up the spiritual universe. Therefore, man, generic man, including all the ideas which go to make up the entire universe of God's creating, must have dominion over the universe of God's creating through and by reason of this reflection.

And thus we find the reason, or authority, for the statement in the Bible that man was given dominion over all the earth. Now, this term "generic man" means one. That is, all the ideas which go to make up the universe and man comprised in one complete whole constitute generic man, or the one complete and only man.

Now, do not become confused by the use of the terms generic man and individual man, or the individuality of man. To make the matter clear, we will say that this one complete, compound idea known as generic man is divided and subdivided into many small compound ideas known as individual man. Each individual consciousness here holds within itself some of the ideas of Mind — that is, it expresses some of the ideas of Mind which go to make up the universe and generic man. So that everything of Truth that you and I reflect in our own individual thinking, constitutes the individual man in us, and all the truth that all of us know goes to make up what is termed generic man. So do you not see that it takes all men to make generic man? That is, it takes all of the individuality in your consciousness and my consciousness and everybody's consciousness to constitute that one complete whole which is termed the one generic man.

Our *individuality* is the amount and variety of true thought present in our consciousness. Our *personality* is the amount and variety of mortal or carnal thinking that claims to have place in our consciousness. The identity of each individuality is that quality of thought which identifies one individuality from another individuality. To explain a little farther: Each one of us here expresses in his or her thinking a little, at least, of the qualities of divine Mind. Each one here expresses, I presume, some degree of Love. Each expresses some degree of purity. Each expresses some degree of spirituality. Each expresses some degree of kindness, gentleness, compassion, wisdom, spiritual intelligence, etc. — all qualities of divine Mind, all ideas of divine Mind. All of those qualities or ideas of Mind which you and I hold in consciousness constitute our individual individuality; and as each one of us expresses more than one of these ideas in consciousness, that combination of such ideas in our make up, in our thinking, in our consciousness, constitutes what Mrs. Eddy refers to as the compound idea — that is, many ideas of Mind compounded in one individual consciousness. The compound idea man means the gathering together in one consciousness of many ideas of Mind. I have gone somewhat at length into this because I have found that often many Scientists are confused as to just what is meant by the compound idea, and also how generic man differs from individual man. Now, generic man and individual man do not differ in quality or idea; they differ simply in quantity or amount. That is, generic man includes all right ideas. Individual man includes a part of the ideas of Mind which constitute generic man. So all the ideas of Mind which go to make up individual man are included in the term generic man. Generic man contains all ideas. Individual man includes only a part.

Proof that God Is Mind

God is Mind, we learn in Christian Science. How do we deduce that God is Mind? By what authority has Mrs. Eddy come to the conclusion that God is Mind and man idea? There are a great many things in the Bible which gives authority for this conclusion or deduction, but there is probably none plainer than that statement in I John, 4th Chapter, where it is written: "He that loveth not knoweth not God; for God is love. No man hath seen God at any time. If we love one another, God dwelleth in us, and his love is perfected in us. God is love; and he that dwelleth in love dwelleth in God, and God in him."

Now, what is love? Is it anything that we can see, feel, taste, smell or hear? Is it anything cognized by the five physical senses? No. It is something you and I express or reflect in our thinking, isn't it? Could you possibly conceive that love could be expressed in any other way than thinking? Outward or physical evidences of love are simply evidences of loving thoughts. An act must be thought before it is put into action or evidence. Therefore, love must be wholly and purely mental, must it not? It must be a product of Mind. It must have originated in Mind.

Now, did you or I ever originate love? Did we ever create love? Why, no. Love has existed eternally. Love has been evidenced through mortals for centuries; and no person, who has ever expressed true love, has originated that love. Love has always been in existence, eternally, and has been possible to all men of all times. Love must have existed long before mortal man ever found a place on this earth, else there would have been no love.

Now, as love must be expressed in thinking and can be expressed in no other way, it must have come from a Mind which has existed long before the so-called worlds were formed. Love exists everywhere, does it not? And can you conceive that Love could ever be exhausted or diminished simply because a great many people express love? If, therefore, as John tells us, God is Love, and if love must be expressed in our thinking, and must have come from some mind, then is there any other conclusion to arrive at than that God is Mind? And is there any other conclusion that one can arrive at except that love is an idea? Therefore, in the proportion that you and I express in our thinking a little of that one idea love, to that extent are we uniting ourselves with Love which is God.

And to just the extent that we are letting thoughts enter our thinking which are unloving and unlovely, to that extent are we separating ourselves from the Mind which creates that great supply of love. The illustration could be carried on indefinitely with other terms, qualities, or ideas of Mind, but this will suffice to show us the utter necessity of making our own union with God through right thinking, and how utterly impossible it is for anyone to think wrongly and still expect the protection, guidance and care which come only from that unity which exists between God and man. The love (to confine ourselves to that one term) which you and I express in our thinking is an idea of Mind. Therefore, when we express love, are we not united absolutely with Mind? Is there any separation between love and the Mind that created it? Now, that love which you and I express in our thinking is the true man in us; it is that part of us which is the image and likeness of God — it is the

Christ in us.

Thus we begin to see what God and His idea, man, are, and how indissoluble the relationship between the two is. It would be inconceivable to think of love as separated in any way from the Mind that created it, would it not? So it would not be possible to think of man, the compound idea of all right ideas, as separated from the Mind that created these ideas. So we can see clearly that back of the real man, or back of these ideas which go to make up the true and perfect man of God's creating, is perfect God.

Spiritual Idea or Material Object

And now we are getting to the point I spoke of a few moments ago of the confusion which has arisen sometimes regarding the spiritual idea and material man. Now mortal man, with all his accompaniments, is a creation of what? Who made, or what made a mortal? Why, you answer, mortal mind. True enough, but where did mortal mind get its pattern for making mortal mind? Did mortal mind get it from God? No, because mortal mind knows nothing about God. Mortal mind would have to be pretty good to come into contact with divine Mind, or God. The Bible tells us, "Thou art of purer eyes than to behold evil and canst not look on iniquity." Therefore, we have Biblical authority for the positive assurance that God knows nothing about mortal mind or material man. Mrs. Eddy tells us in *Science and Health* that if mortal mind knew how to be better it would be better, and she also tells us that the material and the spiritual never mingle and never touch at any point. Therefore there is no possible way to become confused with the supposition that mortal mind ever got near enough to divine Mind to steal its pattern for man and create a man called mortal with the perfect man as a model. In other words, mortal mind never knew anything of God or the man of God's creating, and consequently in making its concept of man, it had to use its own model and could not possibly have used immortal man as a model.

Therefore, while we say, and Mrs. Eddy tells us, that mortal man is the counterfeit of the true, yet we should never become confused with the thought that mortal man is the counterfeit of the spiritual man, with spiritual man as a pattern for the counterfeit. The spiritual man and the material man have no connection whatever as a perfect original and an imperfect copy. Mortal man was never copied from the immortal. In *Science and Health* Mrs. Eddy writes: "Human belief has sought and interpreted in its own way the echo of Spirit, and so seems to have reversed it and repeated it materially." And then she also says: "God creates all forms of reality. His thoughts are spiritual realities. So-called mortal mind — being non-existent and consequently not within the range of immortal existence — could not by simulating deific power invert the divine creation, and afterwards recreate persons or things upon its own plane, since nothing exists beyond the range of all-inclusive infinity, in which and of which God is the sole creator."

It is plain to be seen from the standpoint of reason, and what Mrs. Eddy has given us in all her writings, and from the Bible, that the creations of mortal mind are completely outside the realm of Spirit, and mortal mind has nothing for its own background but its own material conceptions. Therefore, by what authority could you, or I, or anyone else make the assertion, with any degree of understanding of Christian Science, that a spiritual idea is the foundation for a material miscreation? To explain what I mean: Do you say in your metaphysical work, that there is a spiritual idea stomach, or a spiritual idea automobile, or a spiritual idea house? If you do, you have missed the very heart and soul of Christian Science. Many people seem to have become confused in regard to the subject of spiritual idea because of the assertion which has been made that back of every material object there is a perfect spiritual idea. Now, that statement is exactly true. Back of every material object there is a perfect spiritual idea; but that spiritual idea, or those spiritual ideas, have no connection whatever to the material object.

If you could get clear in your metaphysical perception that in place of every material object there is a perfect spiritual idea, or ideas which have no connection with or relationship to the material, then you would be right. You would not say that because there is a material stomach there must be a perfect spiritual stomach somewhere as a background for the material. You would not say that there is a perfect spiritual idea stomach back of the material stomach because that is not so. The material exists, not because of the spiritual, or because mortal mind knows anything of the spiritual. It exists because mortal mind does not know anything of the spiritual and could not create its own creation with the spiritual as a copy. Therefore, what mortal mind says is a material stomach was never created with any knowledge of a spiritual stomach or a spiritual idea stomach.

And I have found out that much confusion in working in the giving of a treatment and in seeing the true spiritual situation in regard to a material condition, exists because of the misconception that the material counterfeit is based upon spiritual perfection. Why do you not see that the moment you try to spiritualize a material object, you have the spiritual as a foundation for the material, and thus you have made Spirit, or God, the author or the creator of all mortal discord, sickness, unhappiness, sorrow and degradation? The moment you try to connect the material with the spiritual, the moment you try to unite them and make one the basis for the other, then you have a dual creation and chaos. What is the truth about any material condition? There is no truth about it. The only truth about it is that it is a lie. It is not a lie about the spiritual. It is a lie of its own creating, and that is all you can say about it.

Correct Handling of Physical Claims

We all know that there is perfect spiritual man, but that does not mean that we can follow that statement with the statement that then there must be a perfect spiritual stomach back of that which mortal mind calls a stomach. If you were called to treat a man for a case which involved his stomach, his lungs, or his heart, would you start in by declaring that that man had a perfect spiritual heart or stomach, lungs, etc.? No, you would not. You would declare that man exists in divine Mind as a perfect spiritual idea; that he is the expression or reflection of God through idea, and that all the ideas of Mind are expressed through man (or patient) in their perfection and their infinity. You would know, among other things, that every function of man, every function of that patient, every faculty of that patient, is a faculty or function of Mind, exists in Mind and is governed, controlled, and directed by that Mind, and that therefore there could be no argument or belief of improper function, superinduced by the belief of torpidity, inaction, overaction, inharmony, of any name and nature that could interfere with the perfect function of man's faculties.

You would take up in your work and handle such arguments as were needed to be handled to meet the requirements of the particular case. If it seems to be a liver complaint, for example, you would handle inaction, torpid action, improper and imperfect elimination, poison which mortal mind says results from inaction or torpid liver, etc. You would know, as I said above, that every function of man, every function of this patient, exists in Mind as a perfect idea in Mind; and is therefore obedient to the Mind that created it; that in Mind there is no inaction or torpid action because all action is here and now perfect in Mind, and that because there is no inaction, or retarded or impaired action, there could be no accumulation of false substance in the form or shape of toxic poison that affect or injure the life of man. You would not pay any attention in your work to liver. Liver is a creation of mortal mind purely and simply, and was never made with a spiritual liver as a model or background.

You would handle the question of substance, action, inaction, improper secretions, improper elimination, torpidity, the argument of poison, etc., from the standpoint of perfect man made in the image and likeness of God. You would not become confused in any way because you would see clearly that there is no matter, no mortal mind, and that man does not live in a mortal body or physical form, and was never in a position or place that God did not put him in, or a condition or environment that God did not create. You would know that spiritual perfection exists right here and now, that this patient was never thrust out of Spirit and was never born into matter, and is therefore not a victim, a child, a slave or a condition of matter; does not live in matter, mortal mind, or a physical body; and because he does not live in matter, he is not subject to any of the laws of matter such as heredity, animal magnetism, or whatever needed to be met in that particular case.

When you have your patient out of matter, then you can know the truth for him on a spiritual basis without any regard to any particular organ or part. There are no spiritual organs. In fact, there are no material organs. There is no material condition to be met. Get your patient into Mind as idea, image, reflection; and then leave him there when you close your treatment, and never let him get out of Mind while you are giving your treatment by becoming confused as to the spiritual idea back of the material. There is no material. All there is, is God and His perfect creation, and in that creation there is perfect action, perfect supply, perfect man, perfect everything, without any reference whatever to the material. Never work from the material. If you attempt to visualize a spiritual organ back of a material organ, you are then working from the material instead of from the spiritual. Never forget Mrs. Eddy's statement that "perfect God and perfect man are the basis of all thought and demonstration in metaphysics," and you will never become confused. Never try to tie the material to the spiritual. The material does not exist. It is a figment of thought — a dream of imagination. "There is no life, truth, intelligence, nor substance in matter. All is infinite Mind and its infinite manifestation, for God is All-in-all. Spirit is immortal Truth; matter is mortal error. Spirit is the real and eternal; matter is the unreal and temporal. Spirit is God, and man is His image and likeness. Therefore man is not material; he is spiritual."

THE INFINITY OF GOD AND MAN

Association Address of 1937

We are all accustomed, in a more or less superficial way, to use the term *infinite* in connection with God, and in our contemplation of Him; but I am sure we do not dwell to the full extent on the meaning of that term in connection with ourselves as reflections of God. Man, in the image and likeness of an infinite God, cannot be localized or limited, as man consists of divine ideas which in themselves express an infinite God. Therefore, man must be the reflection of the infinite nature of God, and could not possibly come under the mortal or carnal thought of localization, circumscription or limitation. God is infinite Spirit. That is, the infinity of Spirit — Spirit filling all space — precludes the possibility of matter anywhere in infinity. Infinity is the only here and now. In other words, there is no here and now in infinity. There is no place in infinity. Therefore, there is no space in infinity, and consequently, all that exists, exists in the infinite, and that means that all creation exists here and now in the consciousness of the ever-present. Because Jesus knew that there was no time, or space, or place in infinity — that there was naught but ever presence — he was enabled instantaneously to transport the ship in which he and some of his disciples had embarked to the other side of the Sea of Galilee.

If God is infinite Spirit, then there is no localized or objectified materiality in existence. In the infinitude of Spirit, there is no matter. Become clear in this. Become clear as to the infinite and therefore the ever present nature of Spirit, to the complete exclusion of all materiality. Spirit — infinite Spirit, God — has His reflection in ideas. These ideas must necessarily express the infinite nature of Spirit. These ideas which express infinite Spirit, constitute man. Hence man expresses infinite Spirit, and could no more be localized or circumscribed than the God which is expressed by those ideas which constitute man. God is infinite Mind, and in the realm of infinite Mind, there could not be minds many or wills many. The sense of infinitude as applied to Mind completely dispels any thought of a multiplicity of minds in the realm of the real. There is but one consciousness, and that is the consciousness of God of His own ideas. Man's consciousness is the reflection of this one infinite Mind; and as man is consciousness, and as the consciousness which constitutes man is constituted of ideas of the one infinite Mind, man can be conscious of nothing but the infinite. He cannot know or sense any argument of localization or limitation or circumscription, as his being is the consciousness of ideas which reflect the one infinite Mind.

God is infinite Truth. As God is infinite Truth, there can be no place for finite or localized error. Error, to become manifested in human experience, has to have a place in which to manifest itself. It has to have a limit in which to deposit itself. It has to have a locality wherein to operate, and an object upon which it may be manifested. None of these things exist in the realm of infinite Truth, where there is no place, no locality, no limit, and no object. Therefore, when you perceive God as infinite Truth without the possible presence of any of these finite qualities of thought, you then have all space filled with infinite Truth wherein is no error at all. And man as the reflection of infinite Truth wherein there is no error, could not possibly be subject to any of the claims of localization, limitation or objectification. If error has to have an object, a place and a locality on which and in which to operate, and man is the expression of that which knows no such thing as person, place, thing, or limits, then man cannot be the subject of localized, objectified or personalized error. Man can be subject to naught that is not included in the divine Mind. So with man as the expression of infinite Truth, and with the exclusion of all error from the realm of infinity, we find man utterly incapable of knowing or expressing error. If you will get clear as to the impossibility of man expressing or being conscious of anything but that which is included in the God-consciousness, you will find the application of Science in your treatments much more effective.

God is infinite Life. In the realm of infinite Life, there could be no death or death process. Man has no life of his own. Man is the expression of that Life which is infinite; and as the sense of infinity brings out the sense of ever presence, man cannot be subject to any finite sense of death or destruction. Life is expressed in infinitude, and the ideas of Life and Truth and Love individually expressed constitute man. Therefore, the consciousness of any right idea in our thinking unites us with the infinite God in which there is no death; and, therefore, every right thought which you and I entertain is eternal Life with us, because a right thought or idea cannot be separated from the infinitude of the Mind which creates it. And in the infinitude of Life, there is no death. We must work under the constant conviction and assurance that our right thinking in any particular is a source of eternal life to us, and that each right thought and endeavor unites us to that infinity in which there is no localization or personalization. Man is not infinite. Man reflects infinity, and is therefore individual. Individual man reflects the infinity of the one Mind, Life, Truth, Spirit; that Mind in which there is not the confusion or arguments of mortality; that Life which knows no death; that Truth which knows no error; and that Spirit which knows no matter.

God is Principle, and God is infinite; therefore Principle is infinite. Principle is the only cause and creator. Principle is that from which all things originate. As a matter of fact, there is no origin in the sense of process. It might better be said that Principle is the source from which all things come or are derived. Everything exists here and now in the realm of the infinite, — complete, eternal, without beginning and without end. A good thought, which comes from or originates in divine Principle, has always existed and will always exist. It never had a beginning, but existed in the divine Mind as a part of that infinite, eternal Mind. Its conscious reflection is man. Reflection might best be expressed as individual consciousness. The individual consciousness of an idea which expresses the infinite is man. Therefore, as God is Principle and is infinite, there can be no conflicting creation or dual creation; and man, as the expression of the infinite, cannot be confused, disturbed or distressed by the claims of a material or substitute creation.

God is Soul, and God is infinite; therefore Soul is infinite. Soul is the consciousness of its own existence to the complete exclusion of any other consciousness. The consciousness of Soul annuls the belief of a confused or an adulterated consciousness. Soul is the consciousness of its own vast system of ideas; and therefore Soul governs these ideas in perfect harmony through its own all-knowing, all-wise and all-seeing intelligence. From this sense of infinite Soul, and man as the conscious, individual expression of ideas reflecting the infinity of Soul, we gain the harmony of man. Man expresses the harmony of Soul, God, and as Soul is infinite, harmony is likewise infinite. Therefore, man is the conscious expression of ideas which express infinite Soul in which there is no inharmonious element, and so he is the expression of infinite harmony. So, every right idea which you and I entertain and express is bringing us into the realm of infinite harmony wherein there is no confusion of thought or purpose, and wherein the one Mind prevails.

God is infinite Love. Man is the reflection, or expression, of infinite Love. As Love is synonymous with the one Mind, and as Love and Mind are infinite, and as there is no other than the one Mind in the realm of the infinite, there could not possibly be room for the presence of hate. Hate could not originate in Love. Hate, like all error, has to have an object. It has to have localities, persons, places, limits; and as none of these conditions exists in the realm of the infinite, man as a reflection of infinite Love could not be conscious of, or the object of localized hate, malice, jealousy, revenge, and the like. There is nothing in the realm of infinite Love in which man lives that could be used as a channel or object upon which hate can operate. Every right thought which you and I entertain, unites us with that infinity wherein there is no hate, and thus are we freeing ourselves from the arguments of malicious mental malpractice and all the beliefs of a mind which claims to be capable of hating.

In the realm of the infinite, there are no boundaries, no localities, no limits, no circumferences, no diameters, no distances, no measurements, no time, no space, and no place, and man is the consciousness of ideas which express the infinitude in which none of these elements of limitation and circumscription exist. So the consciousness of individual man is no more subject to the attacks of the finite than is the Mind, or Principle, from which come these ideas which constitute man's consciousness. Therefore, if you become clear as to the infinite nature of God and man as His reflection, you can clearly see and claim with perfect assurance and certainty that man (and that is yourself) cannot be subject to localized, objectified or personalized error. When you can clearly see how utterly impossible it is for man to become the object or subject of that which does not exist in infinity, then your treatment will be sure, positive and final.

Human Perfection of the Material State

I want to take up with you what I have termed, for the want of a better phrase, "human perfection of the material state." Jesus explained it perfectly when, in giving us what has come to be known as "The Lord's Prayer," he said: "After this manner therefore pray ye; . . . Thy kingdom come. Thy will be done in earth, as it is in heaven."

One cannot think of the kingdom of heaven without gaining some concept of perfection. One thinks of heaven, in fact, as the acme of spiritual perfection. In fact, the kingdom of heaven is the ultimate of all endeavor; it is the Christ enthroned in consciousness to the complete exclusion of all error. The kingdom of heaven is the perfection of Life, Truth, Principle, Mind, Spirit, Soul and Love enthroned in individual consciousness. The perfection of heaven is that beyond which there is nothing, no progress and no goal. So in the contemplation of heaven, we conceive of naught but perfection in its spiritual significance. One realizes, of course, that a perfect spiritual state eliminates completely all matter and material creation or existence. Therefore, to speak of human perfection of the material state might seem a contradiction, but Jesus certainly had some sense of a material condition free from the secondary beliefs of mortal mind, or the carnal mind, when he said, "Thy will be done in earth, as it is in heaven." The will of God in the realm of the spiritual is heaven enthroned. The will of God in the realm of the material must be another thing, and we certainly cannot contemplate the will of God being done "on earth as it is in heaven" without gaining some sense of material perfection from the human standpoint.

It is clear that a consciousness utterly devoid of any sense of God, or God's will, would be quite a different consciousness than the consciousness filled with the love of God. As the outward manifestation, or the physical manifestation, is the product of consciousness — individual consciousness — it is clear that a physical universe which is the object of a human consciousness and which knows nothing of God, or Truth, would be quite a different physical universe from one which is the object of a human consciousness impregnated with an understanding of God. And it also is clear that, as the physical universe is the object of the individual human consciousness, the physical universe in the experience of each individual must gradually improve as individual human consciousness grows in its understanding of God. Therefore the physical universe of an individual whose mind contains no undersanding of Truth, must be quite a different universe for that same individual after gaining Truth and growing in the study and contemplation thereof. That is, a person today who knew nothing of God and the teachings of Christian Science, would look out upon an entirely different world from that which he might see five or ten years hence if in the meantime he has gained an understanding of God through Christian Science.

In the first place, we must gain a clear understanding of the difference between the carnal mind (or mortal mind) on the one extreme, and the divine Mind, or God, on the other extreme, with the human mind sandwiched in between the two. We have dwelt on that thoroughly at one time and another; but to handle the whole question in its entirety, we must take it up again. In *Science and Health*, in her definition of the word Euphrates, Mrs. Eddy says, as a part of that definition, "The atmosphere of human belief before it accepts sin, sickness, or death; a state of mortal thought, the only error of which is limitation; finity; the opposite of infinity." Here Mrs. Eddy recognizes a sinless state of human belief "the only error of which is limitation." By limitation she means circumscription, or objectification — confinement. When she refers to this state of human belief before it accepts sin, she emphasizes the fact that this human belief is a state of consciousness capable of accepting or rejecting carnal or sinful thoughts. She says that this human belief is a state of mortal thought, "the only error of which is limitation." That is, that localization is the only error which characterizes this state of human belief before it accepts sin. Therefore, aside from this claim of localization or limitation, this human belief, or human mind, is sinless. If this human mind should be freed from this claim of limitation or localization before it accepted the arguments of sin, sickness, and matter, it would then be submerged in the divine to the extent that the claim of limitation or localization would completely disappear in pure spirituality.

This human belief, or human mind, which is capable of accepting or rejecting sin, sickness, and matter, gradually takes to itself these elements of the carnal mind which compound and increase themselves until this human mind becomes the possessor of so much of the carnal that it is objectified to the human mind or consciousness as a human body, a material world, sickness, poverty, distress, accidents, degradation, and so on, all of this because of the claim of limitation or localization which denies an infinite God and man in the image and likeness of infinity. The human body is not self-created. It is the mental projection, or objectification of carnal thoughts which the human mind has voluntarily admitted. The human body is not guilty of sin and sickness. It is not the author of the sins and the crimes which it is supposed to commit. It, in itself, is almost as sinless and as blameless as the human mind before it accepts sin, sickness and death.

In *Science and Health*, in the trial found at the conclusion of the chapter on Christian Science Practice, Mrs. Eddy says that in the case of the man who was on trial for liver complaint, "the body committed no offense," and she refers to the body as "the helpless, innocent body" tortured by personal sense operating through false belief. And here is a point which will help you very much in your work of healing — to know that the body is not the offender in any case, and that it simply and innocently manifests that which is imposed upon it by personal sense operating through false belief. Personal sense could be designated as animal magnetism in any of its forms. Do not become confused with the thought that personal sense and mortal man are one. They are not. Personal sense is the claim of mortal mind which operates through the claim of false belief on mortal man or the human body.

So we can conceive of the human body as free from any of the beliefs of personal sense which manifest themselves as sickness, poverty, heredity, and so on. The innocent human body is a concept of the human mind which has not taken to itself those secondary beliefs which manifest themselves as sickness, poverty and the like. I have often quoted this particular passage before from *Unity of Good*, but it is so apropos in this discussion that I shall use it to establish the point I am bringing out. Mrs. Eddy says, "The more I understand true humanhood, the more I see it to be sinless — as ignorant of sin as is the perfect Maker."

It is certain that humanhood, or the human mind, is not the product of the divine Mind. That must be clear to all, and yet she says that the more she understands true humanhood, the more she perceives it to be as sinless as the perfect Maker. Therefore, the human mind, or true humanhood, resolves itself into a state of consciousness, the only distinctive feature of which is localization. It is simply a state of consciousness capable of receiving sin because of its claim to localization. Because of its claim to localization — that is, its claim to existence as a state of consciousness not founded on a sense of the infinite — it is therefore capable of accepting or rejecting that which argues for finity instead of the infinite. That which argues for the finite is bound to be of the carnal mind or mortal mind. Mrs. Eddy says in the definition of Euphrates that the human mind is a state of mortal thought. So, while true humanhood may be sinless, it is, nevertheless, a state of mortal thought; otherwise it would not be and could not be circumscribed and capable of accepting sin, sickness and death.

As this human mind, this state of a localized consciousness, begins to take to itself, at its own volition, carnal thoughts, it begins to build up in consciousness a material world, or universe, which includes all the material phenomena of which you and I are familiar. This universe includes the mortal body, the material universe of which we are conscious, and the hate, anger, jealousy, sickness, poverty, and discord, with which we are daily confronted. Now, if it is possible to conceive of an individual consciousness which has not accepted sin, sickness and death, the only error of which is limitation or localization, it is natural to assume that the process of material salvation would be a process of elimination through the influx of the divine into the human consciousness, even to the point where the human consciousness would have returned to its perfect state of humanhood before complete spiritualization of individual existence can become possible.

To illustrate, let us assume that here is a state of individual human consciousness whose only error is limitation or localization

— circumscription. This human mind or consciousness begins to take to itself thoughts of the carnal mind until it has built up a material universe for itself which includes a material world, a material body, material people. We will assume by way of further explanation, that this material universe and body, which this individual human mind has constructed, becomes complete and mature without any carnal accompaniments of inharmony, sin, sickness, poverty, hate, malice, and the like — a world which, from a human standpoint, would be a perfect place in which to live. Then this human consciousness, takes to itself a larger complement of mortal mind, such as sin, hate, revenge, fear, worry, poverty, old age, decrepitude, dishonesty, fault-finding, incompatibility, selfishness, petulancy, impatience, self-will, human knowledge, the wisdom of material erudition, and the like. All of these various phases of thought are, from the very nature of material existence, included in the universe and body which the individual human consciousness has created before it accepts all of these carnal thoughts.

So we might say, by way of explanation, perhaps, not so much as a matter of fact, that the human mind and its creation involves three steps or stages. The first stage is the human mind without having taken to itself sin, sickness, death and the like. It is the human belief spoken of by Mrs. Eddy in her definition of Euphrates and referred to as true humanhood in *Unity of Good.* Then comes the second stage, or a material universe and a material body unfettered by sin, sickness, inharmony, poverty, and all these besetting ills which make for the misery of human living. Then the third state where the human mind, through the influx of a superabundance of mortal or carnal thought, has endowed this universe and body which it has constructed with all those besetting ills which all of us are daily trying to overcome. Those are the three stages of the human mind in the construction of the world in which you and I live.

This construction is strictly individual. It must be individual because salvation is individual, and because the only explanation of its existence is individual. Carnal thoughts entertained in the human mind create our material world. Carnal thoughts entertained in the human mind endow that world with its sickness, inharmony, poverty and misery. Now, it should be perfectly clear that if the carnal mind, which creates the material world for each individual, could be freed from those thoughts which make that world an unpleasant place for mortals to live in, then the material world, for the individual whose consciousness has been thus set free, would be free from all the claims of inharmony, unhappiness, fear, worry, poverty, sickness and the like. That is, if a human consciousness which had arrived at the third stage of mortality, as above explained, could be free from those thoughts which constitute the third stage of material existence, then that human consciousness would revert to what we have described as the second stage of human consciousness, and the individual would then be living in a world of his own creation, which world would be free from sin, sickness, poverty, inharmony, unhappiness and the like. And this second stage would be what I have heretofore referred to as a state of human perfection. That is, perfection from the standpoint of a consciousness which is still human.

Now, this second state of human consciousness, or the human mind, is arrived at in but one way, and that is through the influx into the human mind of divine ideas which cancel just that much of carnal thought which has heretofore been manifesting itself in our material world. Carnal thoughts are manifested in a material world. Divine ideas, taken into the human consciousness, cancel these carnal thoughts, and thus eliminate that much of the carnal in our world. In this manner, and through this explanation, we are not spiritualizing matter or our material world, but we are spiritualizing thought, and this spiritualization of thought takes away from our world just that much of the carnal, and leaves the balance of our world that much less material.

Our consciousness, for example, has created a world in which there are trees and flowers and vines and water and air and all the elements of nature. This consciousness has endowed certain objects of nature with dangerous, harmful, destructive and even deadly qualities. It creates extremes of heat and cold. It boils the water and freezes the water. It creates our atmosphere. It furnishes the blood which courses through our veins. It endows all the elements of materiality with their distinctive and peculiar qualities. Matter, in itself, is not creative. The poison of the ivy, the irritation of the goldenrod, the sting of the serpent, the carnivorous wild animal, the danger lurking in a draught of fresh air, the infection of the germ, the contagion and the dangers which we find on all sides, are not inherent nor a part of the elements or things through which they claim to act. These destructive and distressing qualities exist only in the human consciousness impregnated with the carnal mind. Neither matter nor the human mind alone is guilty. It is the human mind saturated with carnal beliefs which is responsible for all the inharmonies of mortal existence. In the human consciousness exists our material universe. In the human consciousness also exists those elements of mortality with which we endow our material universe with its inharmonious qualities.

It should be evident that if our human consciousness is freed from those carnal beliefs by means of which we endow our material universe with all its inharmonies, then we would have left a material universe without those dangerous and harmful elements which make for the misery of human living. This can be accomplished only by means of the influx of the divine into the human mind, thus excluding those carnal elements which make for disaster. This is my concept of "thy will be done in earth as it is in heaven." It is a state of human perfection, where love, harmony, peace and the like, reign without any carnal element of inharmony. This is what Mrs. Eddy has termed a "better belief" or an "improved belief," as I have so many times explained.

We can take goldenrod as an example. Allergy to goldenrod is simply a belief of mortal mind, or the human mind, just as is any manifestation of matter. The harmful qualities which we attach to the goldenrod is what we have termed a secondary belief. Now, if through spiritual understanding, we are able to clear consciousness to the extent that the goldenrod is relieved of its distressing features, we have left a concept of the human mind which is not only a "thing of beauty," but "a joy forever." It is still matter, but it is free from harm. It is no more spiritual than the harmful goldenrod, but it is less material. It represents a state of human perfection of the material state. In fact, human perfection of the material state is as necessary a part of individual salvation as is the overcoming of specific and harmful sin. Goldenrod is a belief. Goldenrod without its distressing features is a "better belief" or "an improved belief."

The Millennium in Individual Consciousness

My attention was called the other day to something in *Miscellany* which I had not noticed in connection with the human mind. Mrs. Eddy has stated, "The spirit of the prayer of the righteous heals the sick, but this spirit is of God, and the divine Mind is the same yesterday, today, and forever; whereas the human mind is a compound of faith and doubt, of fear and hope, of faith in truth and faith in error."

In the individual human consciousness is established the true brotherhood of man. One might be inclined to hold to the conviction that the brotherhood of man would depend upon the establishment of Truth in the consciousness of all humanity; that the brotherhood of man could not be accomplished until each and every individual had enthroned God in consciousness. This is not so, any more than the fact that the millennium can arrive only when all mankind is saved through Science. The brotherhood of man and the millennium is established in individual consciousness, because that of which the individual is cognizant through the medium of his senses is the material objectification, or projection, of individual thought. As love becomes enthroned in individual consciousness, all that that consciousness beholds through the medium of the senses becomes lovely. Love enthroned in individual consciousness makes it impossible for that individual to see his brother as hateful, sinful, revengeful, and the like; and thus when love reigns supreme in the consciousness of the individual, then all mankind will become objects of love to the individual. In this way, is the brotherhood of man established in individual consciousness because the brotherhood of man implies man governed by love.

In like manner is the millennium, or the kingdom of heaven, attained. I presume that the average person thinks of the millennium as that state of existence where every individual therein, and every object therein, has come under the rule of divine Mind. If this were so, it would make individual salvation dependent upon the salvation of every individual in the world, and this would take away from one the zeal and prospect of accomplishment. When individual consciousness has become completely spiritual, then will the millennium have arrived for that individual, because one's concept of existence would then have become spiritual, and it is only in individual consciousness that existence of any nature becomes a matter of individual experience. In *Science and Health* Mrs. Eddy says: "Beauty, as well as truth, is eternal; but the beauty of material things passes away, fading and fleeting as mortal belief. Custom, education, and fashion form the transient standards of mortals. . . . Comeliness and grace are independent of matter. Being possesses its qualities before they are perceived humanly. Beauty is a thing of life, which dwells forever in the eternal Mind and reflects the charms of His goodness in expression, form, outline, and color. It is Love which paints the petal with myriad hues, glances in the warm sunbeam, arches the cloud with the bow of beauty, blazons the night with starry gems, and covers earth with loveliness."

It is Love, she says, which makes all things beautiful and harmonious, but where must this Love find expression? Certainly not in the flower whose petals are painted with myriad hues, nor in the sunbeam, which in times of a drought might be the cause of a parched earth, nor in any material object, because, as Mrs. Eddy says, "the beauty of material things passes away." This Love which "paints the petals with myriad hues" and which "glances in the warm sunbeam" must find expression in individual consciousness before it can be manifested as a quality of beauty in the material universe which is the object of our individual thinking. Love does not, independent of individual consciousness, paint the petal with myriad hues. It is the Love in consciousness which does this, and which makes all things beautiful and harmonious.

As individual thought becomes Godlike through the influx of divine Love, the objects of thought, even though materially conceived, become lovely because it would be impossible to separate the objects of thought from that which exists in individual consciousness. For instance, if one held in consciousness hate, or anger, or resentment towards one particular individual, or thing, or condition, that hate could not be separated from everything of which that particular individual consciousness is conscious. That is, the hate or loathing which one might feel toward some particular individual would affect every object in the life and experience of the individual entertaining that hate or loathing. While the objects of individual consciousness may express themselves as many, or as a multiplicity of objects, each object separate and distinct from the other, yet the consciousness, or human mind, through which these various objects become a part of individual consciousness and experience, is one; and the qualities of thought entertained in that one particular consciousness are bound to be manifested in the entire objectification or material externalization of that consciousness. Thus, if your or my consciousness beholds hundreds of different people, and we are entertaining hate in consciousness towards one person, the hate which we hold in that consciousness cannot be separated so that it will not affect everything and everyone of which or of whom we are conscious. We may not be aware that we are hating everyone because we hate one. Nevertheless, we are, and we can never gain the true concept of even our dearest friends and relatives while we are holding in consciousness hate towards anyone. Whatever is held in consciousness affects, in some way or another, every object of that consciousness, be it person, place or thing. Let me quote here a few lines from the pen of one of your fellow students which is very expressive, and which not only is most appropriate in this connection, but which is clear evidence that we may be entertaining angels unawares. The few lines are entitled, "Artists" and are as follows:

A bit of canvas, brush of camel's hair,
Splashes of color from the palette's face,
And ugliness, or beauty's matchless grace
Appear in vivid vision, dark or fair,

A scene from memory, or just a rare
Effect of fancy. Whether pure or base,
Each quality projected has its place
Because the artist's concept put it there.

We are all artists, with uncanny skill
Depicting on the canvas of the thought
Concepts designed to bless us or to curse,
Ours the selection, choosing as we will
The colors of our picture, thus is wrought
Our character, our lives, our universe.

Overcoming Death

In going into this question of death, we must not lose sight of the fact that anything written or spoken on this subject, with the understanding of spiritual existence as entirely distinct from material living, must be founded on the admission that birth, death, (either the first death or the second death) could not possibly be written or said concerning immortal man. Nothing that Mrs. Eddy has given us in regard to death could have anything to do with anything but mortal man. In analyzing what she has said on the subject of death, we must hold constantly to the conviction, based on spiritual understanding, that nothing in this regard could apply to man in the image and likeness of God.

Man was never born and he never dies. He exists as a spiritual identity in the consciousness of divine Mind. Man's own consciousness of himself is the only existence man has. Man's consciousness of himself is his consciousness of divine ideas. Man's concept of himself, or consciousness of himself, is his consciousness of God's concept of man. Nothing that can be said in regard to either the first death or the second death could apply to the man of God's creating.

We have explained the existence of mortal man from the standpoint of the human mind. The human mind is just as fictitious and unreal as the carnal mind, and therefore the creations or the projections of this human mind, through the absorption of carnal thoughts, must be just as unreal and fictitious as the carnal mind or mortal mind. As birth does not apply to God's man, then what might be called "The New Birth" could not apply to God's man. There isn't any first birth. Man is co-eternal and coexistent with God. That applies to you and me here and now. It is the scientific fact of all things that brings freedom.

Material existence, as we all know, is simply the objectification of carnal thoughts held in individual consciousness. Our universe, our environment, our atmosphere, our experiences are all the manifestation of individual human thought. Therefore, the phenomena of material existence is individual. We see matter because we look out from a mind impregnated with carnal beliefs. We see people as material because we see nothing but thought, and thought is material if it comes from the carnal mind. The incidents or events which we see as a part of the lives of those with whom we are associated, exists in our own consciousness. So that when we conceive of a person as dying or dead, we are simply witnessing the externalization of our own thinking. Our carnal thoughts which are objectified to us as the death of a friend, cannot affect the material existence of that friend for the reason that the material world of the friend is just as much the objectification of his mentality as our material world is the individual objectification of our thinking. So, if we see a friend die, that in no way governs or directs the experience of the friend. Death is just as much an individual mental objectification, existing in the mentality of each individual, as is a material object. So that when we think we see a person pass on, our concept of that person does not register in the least that which is happening in the experience of the individual whom we think has passed on.

Our concept of death in no way represents the experience of the individual who has died, or whom we think has died, nor does it change his environment, universe or individual material surroundings. Our material surroundings are simply the individual objectification of our individual thoughts, and our surroundings cannot change until thought changes. Death does not spiritualize the thought of the individual whom we think of as dead, because death is just one more phase of the carnal mind by virtue of which mortals think they live in matter. Inasmuch as each individual makes his own world, experience is likewise individual, and what might be the experience of one would not necessarily be the experience of another under the same conditions. By that I mean that what you and I might look upon as the death of a friend would not, because of our belief, in any way affect that friend. His environment could not be changed because of our belief. His environment could only be changed as a result of a change in his own belief! So what you and I call death does not in any way affect the person whom we think has died, nor does it alter the fact that he dies not. A mortal cannot be rid of mortality through the influences of mortal mind. Therefore, death being a phase of mortal mind, a mortal's material existence is not altered by passing through that experience any more than it is changed by passing through a belief of poverty, sickness, etc.

In an editorial in the *Christian Science Sentinel* of February 3, 1912, there appeared the following: "Earth's pressure of evil beliefs may seem to force the pilgrim to a crucial point of experience, as a phantom frightens into swooning the timid child, and this human crisis in the way heavenward may seem to the unspiritual to be death: but, as to God there is no death, so in Science, to man there is none. What seems to be death is apparent only to those looking on. The individual who knows and loves God, in the transition supposed to be dying, may be more than ever living: living more in Mind and less in matter. When the so-called dead have passed the Rubicon of suffering which is supposed to kill them and to human sense they are seen to be dead, they are not dead. As to the Arctic explorer who has reached the pole, or the point on earth farthest North, there is no North. He can only look everywhere South, even so then to our sense, the dead, having passed the highest point of possible human suffering, find that there is no death, but instead only the dawning of a new and divinely enforced sense of life."

The following is attributed to Mrs. Eddy: "Death is not in the victim whom we say has died, but in us. It is we who are still alive as we term it; it is we who dig the grave; it is we who put our friends into the ground and forever afterwards declare them gone. All these phenomena are in us, not in them. Our verdict of death upon our friends does not change them one iota. Jesus was the same after apparent death and burial as before." Mrs. Eddy once said: "If you were sitting in a chair and an archer should come to a window and send an arrow to your heart, you would feel a shock — a commotion — nothing more. You would try to continue conversation — but finding that you could not do that, you would try to find those with whom you could converse, while I would have to bury the body which I saw in the chair."

Now, you and I can do anything we want to with our concept of the body of a friend who has died, or seemed to us to die; in fact, we could even cremate his body; but that would in no wise affect or appertain to our friend's concept of his body, because in cremating our concept of his body, we have in no way touched or changed his mentality, and in his own individual mentality exists his own material body, and nowhere else. His seeming material body is not matter. It is thought — his thought — just as our concept of his material body is our individual thought, and not his. Now, at this point let me quote from a question asked by a member of the Association. He says: "If our existence is individual, and it is, and we make our own world which accompanies us in death and there is no change for us, how will we ever be united with those who have gone on? Our present state does not include their presence, hence if death works no change, we certainly won't be with them again. Yet, Mrs. Eddy says we will, in numerous instances, and in addition has written a poem about the meeting of her departed mother and husband."

This question, while a natural one, would lead me to believe that I have not yet made it clear to all of you that existence and the phenomena of material existence lies only in individual human consciousness, and that nothing can happen or become an object of individual experience that is not the result of individual belief. This question asks how we are going to be able, after death, to join those who have gone before, if those who have gone before have not been a part of our environment before we pass on. Have I failed to make it clear to you that even the phenomena of the passing on of a friend is a phenomena of our individual consciousness, and that therefore if we believe that someone has passed on to another plane of existence, this incident is merely a creation of our own thinking and the separation is one of thought only?

In our present state of material existence the belief that one person has passed on is just as much a part of our mental objectification as is the belief that another person of our acquaintance has not passed on. The two conditions exist in individual consciousness only. Therefore our present state of consciousness includes not only the belief that our friends exist here and now with us in the flesh, but it also includes the belief that they have left us, and that when we die we shall join them in that existence to which they have gone. The same belief of our individual consciousness which tells us that our friends have passed on also tells us that we shall some day pass on. Therefore, if our separation from our friends lies only in our individual belief about them and the incident of their passing, is it not clear that as soon as this same human belief takes us through the same experience and we find out that we have not died, as they have found out through their experience that they have not died, we shall find ourselves in the same state or plane of thought that they found themselves on awakening from the belief of death, and through this belief, we shall find ourselves freed from the belief of separation? The separation lies only in our individual belief about it. If this belief changes through either our own death, or through our individual spiritual perception, the belief of separation is destroyed, and the old belief of association exists. All there is to material, personal separation is belief. If the belief of material, personal separation is overcome one way or another, then there appears again the belief of material, personal association.

This brings up the question as to what is meant by "the second death has no power." I believe that this is fully covered by Mrs. Eddy's statement in *Science and Health*, as follows: (Marginal Heading: 'Second Death') "Existence continues to be a belief of corporeal sense until the Science of being is reached. Error brings its own self-destruction both here and hereafter, for mortal mind creates its own physical conditions. Death will occur on the next plane of existence as on this, until the spiritual understanding of Life is reached. Then, and not until then, will it be demonstrated that 'the second death hath no power.'"

From this it would appear that the "second death" of which she speaks has to do with material existence after what is termed death. As I said before, we must be clear in our understanding that anything that is said in connection with death has to refer only to material existence and its attendant phenomena. It could have no reference whatever to immortal man, because immortal man has no connection with, or reference to, material man. Therefore, both the first death and the second death must refer to material existence before and after what is termed death.

Clearly the first death with which a mortal is confronted is the death of the material body. That death may be accomplished in one of two ways: It may be accomplished by the individual passing on as mortal man in the experience of what you and I term death. It may be accomplished through translation of the individual from the material to the spiritual by means of pure spiritual understanding. In either case, we have what is termed the first death. St. Paul speaks in one of his epistles of "dying daily," meaning by that the overcoming of carnal beliefs through spiritual understanding. This dying daily would or could be termed the first death, although one's spiritual understanding might not be sufficient to have accomplished the translation at the time of death.

Of course, if one were spiritually clear enough to be able to overcome matter entirely without going through the experience of death, it is evident that he would never again come under the claim of death. Mrs. Eddy tells us that as long as we live in a material state, even though that material state continues after what we term death, we shall be subject to the claim of death until we overcome the claim through spiritual understanding. By that I take it to mean that unless one becomes sufficiently spiritually-minded to overcome the claims of matter and death, he will be subject to death as often as his experience presents that condition, and that might be many times and throughout time indefinitely.

If one, through spiritual understanding, overcomes the belief in matter sufficiently to have overcome matter, then that would be called the first death, and naturally, one would not be subject to a subsequent claim of death, and obviously there would be no second death, and thus the second death would have no power. In one place in her writings Mrs. Eddy says that to those who pass on with enough spiritual enlightenment, the second death will have no power. By that I assume she means that even though we have not arrived at the stage where we have been able to overcome death entirely in the first instance, yet if we pass on with sufficient spiritual understanding, then the experience through which we pass will sufficiently clarify consciousness so that the demonstration of complete dominion will be made without any further experience along that line. When Jesus told Nicodemus that he "must be born again," he was bringing out the fact that in order to enter into the kingdom of heaven, or spiritual existence, Nicodemus must regenerate consciousness to the point where matter would be overcome through spiritual understanding.

The experience of rebirth is what you and I are undergoing hourly. In order to put off matter with its claims to mortality and death, each one of us must be mentally born of Spirit, and that, of course, is an individual undertaking. I would not say that human or material birth is the death referred to as the first death. And I would not say, from what Mrs. Eddy has written on this point, that our present material existence is a state of "probation after death." The only death which could possibly constitute the first death would be the death of what we call matter or the material body. There could be no death before that time because material existence does not represent anything but an individual state of consciousness. It has no connection with the real man and is not a perversion of spiritual Life, because Life cannot be perverted. By concluding that material birth is the first death and material existence is the state of "probation" after death, we are assuming that material existence has something, somewhere, to do with spiritual existence and its misstatement by mortal man. The real and spiritual Life of man is never changed; it is never touched by the material sense of life; and material birth is in no way a misstatement of spiritual Life, nor does it interfere with the real existence of the individual.

Mrs. Eddy points to Jesus' experience in the tomb and his resurrection from the grave with the same material body that he had before death, as proof of a "probationary state beyond the grave." This probationary state, she points out clearly, is the state of existence which a mortal experiences after he has passed through what is termed the first death. As I see it, there might be any number of what would be called "second deaths" for a mortal who had never reached a state of spiritual understanding sufficient to free him from the belief of matter. Clearly, Mrs. Eddy's reference to the first death is that which mortals experience at the end of what we call material life, and the second death is that which we experience as a part of our existence after what we term death. Keep in mind that material existence, the first death and the second death, and the state beyond the grave are simply individual mental phenomena which have nothing to do with our state of spiritual existence. Mortal man is not spiritual man gone wrong. Mortal man and all the phenomena of material existence through death and thereafter, is a mental illusion. When we, through spiritual enlightenment, awake from the illusion, we will find our true status as unfallen children of God.

Everything that you will ever accomplish in Christian Science will be the result of your individual prayer. Immerse yourself in prayer. It is not necessary to always direct your work to a particular end or for a definite outlined purpose. Prayer consists in a clear realization of what God really is and of man's condition as His expression. Contemplate on this, long, seriously, consecratedly, without reference to matter, mortal man, individual problems, and the like. Immerse yourself in the realization of the complete wholeness of Deity and His reflection. The nothingness of matter cannot come as a complete conviction until the wholeness of Spirit is mentally attained. You cannot work against matter or material conditions. You do not do your mental work to realize the nothingness of matter. Your work is to establish in consciousness the allness of Spirit and spiritual ideas, and this automatically and conclusively establishes in consciousness the nothingness of matter. When you can unsee matter and realize man as existing distinct and separate from what is called the mortal body and a material environment, you can then make those declarations of Truth with a conviction that will heal the sick.

ABOUT THE AUTHOR: William Duncan Kilpatrick was a native of Owosso, Michigan. He graduated from Olivet College in 1895, and from the University of Michigan with the degree of LL.B. in 1898. He practiced law for two years in Owosso, and from 1900 to 1907 in Washington, D.C., after which he was in the land and lumber business for several years.

Mr. Kilpatrick became interested in Christian Science in 1899, and became a member of The Mother Church in 1905. The same year he had primary class instruction. Several years later he left the business world, and entered the public practice of Christian Science in 1912.

For three consecutive years he was appointed Committee on Publication for Michigan. He left this work in 1917 upon election to membership on the Christian Science Board of Lectureship. Except for periods taken for the study of Christian Science, he lectured continuously in the United States and abroad until July of 1944. He became a teacher in 1919, holding his class and Association each year in Detroit.

He was made head of Committees on Publication at The Mother Church, The First Church of Christ, Scientist, in Boston, Massachusetts in July, 1944, and was serving in that capacity when